MERRIE LYNN ROSS

Life as an IMPROV'

HAHA Healers Series

Library of Congress Control Number

ISBN 09827366-1-4

Ross, Merrie Lynn

Life As An Improv'/Merrie Lynn Ross

ISBN 978-0-9827366-1-6

Printed in the United States of America.

CONTENTS

Dedication ii

Introduction ....

Chapter1   Game Changers 1

Chapter2   Bring Happy Home- Living The Folly .. 17

Chapter3   Way To Worthiness - Heal The Hurts 29

Chapter4   Be Happy With ….................................. 51

Chapter5   Lighten Up - Flow...... 75

Chaptere6 Life As An Improv' It Is, Ya' Know 95

              ....

Chapter7   MerrieWay Q & A 127

           Additional Resources 131

           About The Author 133

           Byron's Gift.. 134

Salutation.. 129

GRATITUDE

Thank you to all of the generous Souls, who have shined their heart's joy and laughter to live an uplifting life.

To my teachers, mentors, friends, and workmates, too many to mention, you know who you are, who have helped me to see life as a full cup of wonder.

To the funny ladies and gents, who bring laughter into our soul, to heal and rally through pain, hurt, and disappointments.

Especially to my endearing Mother Betty, who taught me to be gentle of heart when trekking this Earthwalk. To save the fry-pan for the kitchen, instead of smacking people with my truth, while blasting through this precious life. Oops... even if I don't follow it sometimes. She also taught me 'to thine own self be true'.

DEDICATION

Byron, my beloved son, at 16-years-old directed his first film, HAHA Gang at Valley College. He fashioned Laughter as a healing technique. The cast of flamboyant actor's gathered in our living room and the chuckles began. The hilarious day was filled with light heartedness, camaraderie, and Byron's loving spirit.

Astounded by Byron's awesome creativity, spontaneity, and improvisational talent, I asked, him "Where did those funnies come from? He flashed a mischievous grin, then he began laughing so hard, tears streamed down his face. We all caught the contagious uproar. Finally he chuckled, "Mom, you potty trained me with funnies, clowning around, remember?" Again the room lighted with laughter, happy hearts, and pure joy.

HAHA Healers emerged from HAHA Gang, your directorial creation, you gifted us with...on that memorable day. Heartfelt gratitude for sharing and including All of us... in your blessed...magical world. My precious Byron, your early departure from this world at only 22...has left me tender, raw, overflowing with your immeasurable love. Your wish for me... remains my eternal quest... to "BE Real, Laugh & Love...

Merrie Lynn Ross

INTRODUCTION

"Do As I'm Wishing… Not As I Doing."

Life IS An Improv'…or you would have been born with a script in your hand. And, since you weren't, it's about time to get with the TRUST program. Trust is a major factor in improvisation, as in life, since you don't know what's coming next, or what the other actor's will say or do. Number one you have to trust yourself, not to anticipate, think ahead, or try to figure it all out. A space of allowing 'what is there' emerges. You open to life's adventure, spontaneously flowing, responding without preconceived notions. Slapstick, pratfalls, pie in the face, and slipping on a banana becomes a free-for-all, contagious hilarity, joyous...and Freeing.

AHA! Improv' is in play when you Listen from your core of BEing, without anticipating results. In calm repose, you observe behavioral nuances and verbal innuendoes with every cell in your body. The five senses are totally alert, sounds, touch, smell, sight, and the sixth sense - intuition guides the way.

Happy's # 1 Sense is HUMOR, everything lightens up as NON-Sense, and we end up with Real COMMON- Sense.

YES in the Improv' brings the element of wonder into play and every moment is new. Childlike curiosity keeps the scene fresh, exciting, unexpected. Fixed beliefs and judgments drop... no good or bad, as discovery unfolds. A 360-degree awareness, anchors you with the other players, with commitment, and total immersion in the Action.

Improv' puts you in a FLOW state... where you Fearlessly seize the moment without resistance. A sense of ONE-ness ensues, an altered state of the comedy zone. You feel as if you're operating as ONE in the group, egoless, and with total trust in each other.

'NO...is a no-no, unless there is a play on words. NO, stops the action, giving no space to move forward. "YES" is the operative word, agreement is the basis of comedy. There is agreement to disagree.

'YES is an open attitude, an overall intention...that promotes the Funnies. Similarly in life when we're open and receptive we feel lighthearted. Given our best planning, we can't control every circumstance, and even the best soothsayer misses in predicting the future. No way out, we must learn to trust our self. When we trust our inner core a portal of opportunity opens, synchronistic events occur, beyond our wildest dreams.

Opening to "YES our childlike wonder brings on the joy. Now is your time to enter the world of "Life As An Improv." To lift off your rigid stance, to drop judgments, release fixations, 'always doing things one way'. Awareness expands...you can heal a lifetime wounds and step into the life you born to live. HAHA Healers brings on the Laughter, the spirit of inner Knowing.

Crack the Happiness Code... To BE Real Laugh & Love.

CHAPTER 1

♥ GAME CHANGERS ♥

As a child I was enamored with anthills. They would appear out of nowhere on our front lawn. Hours would fly by as I watched little ants gathering in methodically orchestrated lines, carrying super loads on their backs, heading to the hill. One day as a mound of carefully laid dirt peaked at its highest, a group of ruffian boys raced by and stomped it into oblivion. My heart plummeted at the devastation, as the little ants' scurried 360 degrees, in chaos. Somewhere ancient memories tucked away inside of me flashed the horror of the downfall of cities, civilizations, warfare's senseless obliteration and destruction.

The next morning the ants were up and at it, building a new hill, not affected by the earlier disaster they continued on without fear of past memory. Taking their effort as a cue, I rallied the ruffians to observe the ants busy at work. I shared my dismay about their lack of awareness of the ant's plight. I endured their jests and teasing and finally I knew they heard me. I explained that this would be a good exercise for them to consider the ants as an example of what the world was about…Peace or War.

Lesson To Learn: I contemplated how I could make the world a better place. In that moment I decided to become a contributor in this life…to take only what I needed and to forfeit becoming a glutton on the planet.

Overtime, this philosophy trickled into relationships and instead of only viewing my needs I became more aware of what other people needed to feel secure. So many small decisions or dilemmas seem to feel like 'do or die'. I often contemplate the anthill destruction, and continue to remind myself that my world is not falling apart when my car engine blows up or my hair starts falling out from a toxic product.

Improv' Tips: This practice is simple: Be aware and truthful. If a situation seems to be devastating, ask yourself. "Is the anthill really crumbling or am I overreacting and dramatizing?

♥ If so, why are you spending time to be upset? Is this a habit? Are you comfortable with chaos?

♥ Who modeled it? Do you like the attention you get when you are in chaos? Remember: Out of chaos Creation is born, in each moment, each breath is creation in action.

♥ Go gentle with yourself, remember: It takes patience to develop a new skill. Aha! Too much patience leads to... Procrastination.

Human dynamic... Frequency of the Improv'

The Real You, the authentic one living full-blast with purpose is born with a potential factor - no limits to evolve to your optimum. Each one of us can be inspired by the likes of Einstein, Mother Teresa, or George Washington, each exemplifying their innate talent, extraordinary accomplishments, and living the life they were born to live.

All of our circumstances and innate potential are unique unto our selves. No fair comparisons, we are each challenged to go the distance... If you are born with a severe leg deformity your destiny is clear in some respects, you are guaranteed not to become MVP champion in the NBA, nor will you win the 100 yard dash in high school. Short of that, your innate talents are fair game to be developed. It then boils down to passion, perseverance, and ATTITUDE. You choose to live the life you love... you are free.

Technicolor Zone

Inner dialogue Living life in Technicolor is: I am worthy of my good. My life matters. "I can do it" I follow my inner calling and do the things that inspire me. I am not in conflict with growing, expanding into the wonder of my divine self. I listen to my intuition and follow my own heart. In spite of other's opinions, I honor what is right for me. I operate from the place of self-love I can truly love other people and serve the highest good for all.

In the Technicolor zone, the optimum attraction for our good is in play, no matter what we do... we do it full out. We jump into opportunity and we honor our uniqueness, our passion, our preferences, and we feel entitled to have it all. The 'all' circumvents what society says is 'cool' - the newest car, hair color, or profession to pursue. The All is 'what turns you on', what you savor in your soul. You choose beneficial actions that resonate at your core of BEing, you are comfortable in your own skin.

Grey Zone

Inner dialogue in the grey zone. Gag me. I forgot what turns me on. Maybe nothing. My life is reduced to hum-drum, work, worry, get the kids o school, cook, eat, sleep. Same old stuff.. I'm trapped, suffocating.... in the midst of my life... everything seems blurred, I don't see a possibility of change. This is my lot in life.

In the grey zone, you settle for . Your consciousness is dim about 'who and what you truly are.' You bought into a herd mentality, 'don't make waves, be odd, or different. Fitting in and being accepted supersedes authentic living. Keeping the status quo is a comfort zone, rather than risking change, facing challenges or conflicts. In your boredom, not reaching out for your potential, settling on mediocrity... a part of you remains anxious waiting for the shoe to fall.

Black & White...

Black and White Zone inner dialogue. My way is the only way to live. I will fight for what I want and pay the price. If someone stands in my way, I can overpower them or leave. I don't need anyone who is against what I feel is right. Follow me or else. The Black and White Zone. is an old fashioned life snapshot, it's stifling, limiting, and an up and down emotional roller coaster ride. You cling to fixed, rigid ways of living your life by following dogma, fixed beliefs, "I'm right you're wrong stance, overriding common sense and balance. In the black and white zone, you need control, you struggle, battle for your needs, needing to be top dog, and to live in your perceived boundaries. Either you feel on top or you are a victim. The chronic undercurrent, everything will fall apart is I let go, I must hold on no matter what, or I will not be OK.

Unlike the Grey Zone, life is not hum-drum, your Black and White world is filled with drama and confusion when things don't go as planned or how you want them to be. You may feel alone and isolate to hide your feeling or resentment, pain, and disappointment.

The zones are not carved in stone, we may vacillate from one to another in different areas of lives. We may live in the Grey Zone when it come to our career, or live in the Black and White Zone in our love relationships. In a patriarchal society we may feel 'right' being a dominating male or succumbing as a subservient woman. Our worthiness or entitlement may be eclipsed by ethnic or familial upbringing. Yet we may simultaneously live in Technicolor in our hobbies, playing tennis, or having fun with our children. The awareness of where you are stuck, living robotically, will help you to make empowering changes into full-blast living.

List the ways you are living in Technicolor, the Grey zone, or in Black and White. What would be beneficial for you to change? What attitudes, beliefs, or habits are blocking you? Pick one to change right now. Begin with a first step. Clean your closet, locate your estranged brother, see a counselor. What are the things you could add, the things you love to do, or a quality you would like to cultivate, leading to the Technicolor Zone?

Merrie Lynn's Giggle

As daytime's first comedienne I had my taste of 'giggling' my way into the hearts of millions of viewers on "General Hospital." I created a 'giggle' for Emma Lutz, my character. It became my trademark and changed my life. I received truckloads of mail, mostly saying the same thing, "Merrie Lynn, whenever I think of you and your giggle, I smile and feel happy."

What would life be without a laugh, a giggle or a yahoo? As a comedy player my whole life has been surrounded by a laugh track. And that includes my brother, my son; even my dog shines a big smile and wags his tale to prove it. How does this play out during these times of a pandemic of 'doom and gloom'? My heart often whispers, "I wish I were on the moon." Staying upbeat is more challenging than ever. When I'm hurting, sad or melancholy, even a crow squawk is a sign to switch to a happy gear. Finding sweet moments as a habit is an instant mood-changer, to be merrier, more flowing, and worry-free. Watching funny movies can turn a sourpuss into a happy face. I choose to laugh often. It's a habit you can choose. Byron's HAHA Laugh Track puts a bounce in your step and a Smile on your face.

♥ BYRON'S HAHA LAUGH TRACK ♥

In honor of Byron and his HAHA Gang...let's not waste another precious second. Let's laugh to the heavens ...with the HAHA Laugh Track.

♥ Begin Repeating HAHAHA...Keep it going. Fake it, until it is uncontrollable.

♥ Laugh it up with family, friends, coworkers, and pets, in the Mirror.

♥ Make HAHA's your daily treat. Do IT! Watch how your mood uplifts.

♥ Can't worry and laugh at the same time. Spread

Humor is a proven anecdote to pain. It's a healing agent that diffuses stress, anger, frustration, and misunderstanding. Emma's 'giggle' spilled into my daily, making me appreciative of its power... to live a healthier, happy life.

Kindness Is Love In Action

Kindness is an inside job…how you treat yourself, the thoughts you have, how you describe yourself to others. Words are powerful. Speaking or thinking a word impacts your experience, affecting those around you. While Thinking or saying," I'm stupid". I'm no good. I'm miserable" change the game and say, "I'm growing. I'm strong. I'm joyous." Remember suggestive Words are powerful. They impact equally strong vibrations, whether positive or negative, and permeate our existence. Your subconscious mind is waiting for directives; you are the boss, giving it input and information. Choose your thoughts and statements wisely. Be wary what words people say about you, discriminate their validity.

Acts of Self-Kindness:

♥ Get past praise or blame.

♥ Don't take everything personally.

♥ Allow zingers to wash over you.

♥ Don't allow words to boost you up or do you in…consider the source, the intent, and if you sincerely value the opinion.

Tongue Twisters are mood altering, mind benders. Repeat: Peter Piper picked a peck of Pickle Peppers, Where's the peck of pickle peppers Peter Piper picked.

In the Improv' world there is no predictability or expectation of results...the skill serendipitously spills over into daily life and an appreciation of the unexpected occurs. A lighthearted attitude helps to cope with personal and global heaviness, during these times of upheaval, chaos, and change. In my book "Bounce Off the Walls – Land On Your Feet", I include Improv' skills to Morph Havoc & HAssles into HArmony & HAppiness. Each word begins with HA and they are our HAHAHA'S.

Let's go for Giggles, Laughter, Guffaws'...great for body, mind, and soul.

♥♥♥

On "Happy Days" I played a character named Bubbles La Rue. I giggled my dimples into a groove. Then I grew into Emma Lutz, a throw back to Jean Harlow in "Dinner at Eight" struggling to get into high society. In one very awesome event...the two shows met on the baseball field for a playoff game for physically challenged kids. There comes a time when we are at the right place at the right time to learn life lesson.

Awesome to go up against my buds, Henry Winkler and Ron Howard. Tony Danza appeared out of now where with Cher and Bill Cosby. Bill orchestrated the mood, how we would allow fair play for the kids. I played shortstop to Cosby's pitching. He is the best with kids; he'd toss the ball backwards to allow the runners to get on base. I would drop the ball, players would fumble, juggle balls in the air, and we all had a wonderful time. I learned about winning, losing, and the ultimate meaning of being a good sport. Bill Cosby claimed the moment of truth...the children were stretching every belief just to walk let alone run the bases.

The kids courage and fortitude became a touchstone for me that day. "Stop whining, complaining, making excuses." The bar raised, nothing measured up to those kids who gave their all. If we give less than our all, living in excuses, we'll miss the joy of just playing the game.

Born to Win

"Complain, complain! How else to get what I want?"

Your are Born to Win. Winning is an inside job that reflects outward in your life experience. At the most base level...we win because we breathe. We are born winners, alive to thrive. When we pop out of the womb, the game begins. From suckling to chuckling, from testing to resting...all boils down to 3 things.

♥ Find the game you love, play with all your heart.

♥ Go the distance to give your best, practice skills to be the best you can be..

♥ Then it's a let-go, a journey into the mystery of the unknown... odds, chance, per chance to dream...the Big Win! Rebirthing yourself... As YOU!

Heal & Bounce Into Freedom

How to muster courage? Courage comes when we have nothing left to lose...during a trying time, a divorce, loss of a loved one, lost dreams, chronic illness…when life is no longer the same. We can't go on pretending, existing in the same mode of being. We are propelled to see 'what matters'...we shift into Knowing, recognizing what really counts. There is no going back. Everyday masks we wear to get through unscathed, good guy, bad girl, adorable, a victim -- drop. We SEE clearly, beyond the limited veil of illusion... the trappings that hold us back from connecting to the bountiful life we are meant to embrace and enjoy. Contemplate, what is the life you are meant to live? Sometimes, it's easier to know what you are unhappy with and how and why you settle for a half-mast existence. The unrest you feel, the uncomfortably, the misery, may be your soul's call to change directions, into the Light of your Soul's intent.

Juggling Mind's Folly

"If its' all in my head, what's in yours?"

The mind 'Plays Tricks' constantly, convincing you it is your master, manipulating that every little thought you have, is true, and that every feeling you have is who you are. This is illusion, the veil of ignorance that traps you in delusion. You give our power to someone else, or some circumstance experience believing it is REAL, often an erroneous perception, and we continue on controlled by false belief. Nonsense, the mind is not our Master! Our Being connects and IS the source of ONE illumined with infinite intelligence. YOU are the creator, connected the connected to infinite possibilities. You are in control of what we think, say, and do.

But, you don't believe that? You want to be taken care of; you want someone to love you…to show you his or her Love first before you express that Love. We are so afraid of our pain, that we reject the opportunity to experience true joy and love. We fake it, sublimate with addictions, loneliness, knowing deep inside we are not authentic. Masquerading and hiding, we forget our original intent for taking on this life...our reason for being here, our purpose to discover and share that Love.

Imagine Being Free

No one can prevent you from seeking your highest purpose. No One, other than YOU can Know your Truth. Resting in that space of wonder, gives right answers, melts resistance and fears. You muster courage, with the Intention to accelerate bountiful and joy-filled living.

How To Free Children?

"Give me the parents & the children are cared for." Baba

We don't give freedom to anyone...our journey is to live authentically, to discover, unravel our own truth of BEing. Freedom is internal and expresses through flow of actions, synchronicity of meetings, events, propelled from Source, from what is right for you, in a particular time and space.

Sometimes we can be self-sacrificing; putting other's needs before our own. We must imbibe the practice of nurturing ourselves before we can effectively nurture our spouse, children, or anyone else. As Mothers and Fathers, many of us would give our life to save our child. We are wired to protect, it's in our DNA, mama and papa bears. When our children grow older giving space, honoring them, and letting go, trusting they will learn their lessons and ultimately BE OK...is a parent's greatest challenge. Blessings to all the mama, papa, & baby bears for their courage.

In the same way, we must 'choose' to let go of what we don't need. To let go of beliefs, relationships, and psychic debris no longer serving us. To let go simply means to accept what "IS now. What is troubling you now, is the challenge before you...to accept and change it, if it can be changed. "To change what you can change NOW." And to accept 'What it is' that you cannot change. No matter how many times I hear this creed...until I choose to live it I won't own it. Can you accept 'what is'?

Self-reliance is a piece of freedom. That doesn't mean living in a vacuum, doing and baring everything alone. Self-evolvement includes learning to ask for what you need, knowing you are entitled and worthy. Hiding in a shell out of embarrassment, shame, or unworthiness limits potential. Living in self-denial, suppressing what serves you, ignoring what you want, what you can imagine is the polar opposite of being REAL and true to yourself.

To BE Real

♥ Awareness that you are not the body, mind, or emotions.

♥ Listen to your 'inner voice', the witness of all external and internal experience.

♥ Observe the 'Witness state within'...see your physical body, mind, and emotional body as vehicle to express Source of Being... the REAL ONE...that you are.

Witness State of Being. Contemplate the notion.

♥ Who is it that hears your thoughts?

♥ Who is it that sees and hears your dreams?

♥ Who is it that feels your anger, joy, or loving moments?

♥ Who is the Watcher, the ONE that is always with you?

"I AM THAT"

CHAPTER 2

BRING HAPPY HOME
♥ LIVING THE FOLLY ♥

Mindful Action – For Problem-Solving

"Mama said there be days like this...only she didn't say I'd be in them."

What we see in our lens of vision can create overwhelm. In this time of accelerated internal and external change requires mindfulness, an alert observation of what we see and feel. Caught in global devastation occurring on so many fronts, from our sea creatures struggling for breath of life, our wounded warriors coming back from senseless war, human sex trafficking, escalating teen suicides to financial devastation.

When we feel general overwhelm our sleep patterns are interrupted and daily negative thinking wraps a cord, binding our state of BEing. We are left with restlessness, anxiety, sadness, and an inept feeling of how to respond. We are frozen in doomsday time, robbed of motivation to progress toward a positive future. Albert Einstein left us a key to unlock this negative future lens viewing, he said, "Imagination is everything. It is the preview of life's events."

What's Troubling you? Uplift Thru

Imagination's Lens.

♥ Sit quietly for a moment; breathe into a space of Stillness.

♥ Become aware of what is troubling you. A project uncompleted, your child's well being, whatever feels stuck festering inside of you.

♥ Envision how you would choose the outcome to be. Allow all possibility to flow without editing or judgment.

♥ In this state of possibility, notice how you feel. Are you less anxious, dissolving overwhelm?

Developing Imagination with the 7-Step Morph process is the backbone of Merrie Way Community's programs, working with youth. "Morph America" & "Peace Smarts" curriculums combine imagination and logic for problem solving issues of concern.

"My actions are infinitely energized… I live in my full potential." This awareness prepares you to take the first steps with a fresh perspective: An upliftment to life's tasks.

Mark Twain & Me

"My imagination is working overtime. Wish I could remember where I put it."

Maybe its because I grew up on the street Mark Twain…that I believed I could travel very far, in my mind that is. I could imagine and fill my hours with delightful experiments, from examining anthills, catching tadpoles in the pond, to flitting after fireflies under the night sky. And being a brat whenever I had a chance, added to the emotional mystery that lingered within me. No I wouldn't! I promise I wouldn't eat a creepy-crawly in a bun. But being mischievous and doing a little fibbing, spinning a wild tale made life more exciting… to a child of eight.

And maybe I loved being left-handed because Einstein claimed to be…or because it seemed so special. As time marched on, no matter how hard life seemed to hit me, a sad divorce, even sadder breaking up a family…the family I longed for and felt so whole to be a part of. Somewhere deep inside, I knew I could travel far in mind, and I could discover the magic in the day. The four-leaf clover waiting to be discovered, the luck of discovering a new trail on a hike, or the laugh-out-loud resonating from my son's room.

And maybe when a friend stroked my face and asked, "What's up?" the tender caring brought a glint of tears in my heart. I guess I knew then it was 'All About Me' and it was time to get on with it...on to discovering the magic in the day and the tranquility in the night. Yes! That I choose.

Maybe it's because you grew up chasing rainbows, and lighting matches when you shouldn't have, or finding a secret hide-out in the bush that makes you so special.

I can imagine stroking your face and asking, "What's up?" You deserve the caring tenderness. It's OK to say, "All About Me"...and to discover the enlivened tingle in your heart, the surrender to whatever is keeping you from discovering...the magic in the day and the tranquility in the night. Can you choose that NOW? Can you say, YES?

♥♥♥

Banish Loneliness, Anger, Worry with Laughter. Being daytime's first comedienne on General Hospital, during the heyday with Liz Taylor, Demi Moore. John Stamos and famed, Luke and Laura, I created a giggle was infectious. Stacks of fan mail affirmed, "Love your giggle", "When I see or think of you I smile...it brightens my day." My secret, "Every time I giggle it brightens my day."

Laughter As A Healing Agent

As mentioned, my beloved son, Byron's first film was the "HaHa Gang". Our living room was filled with laughing students, so contagious that I couldn't stop laughing, even when he said cut.

This preceded the Yoga Laughter Craze. Enthralled with how Byron originated the HAHA Gang I asked what motivated him. Thoughtfully he replied, "When you Laugh you are Love itself...no barriers inside or outside yourself. You are Free." In Byron's enlivened memory we created HAHA Healers.

♥♥♥

On overwhelm, anxiety ridden, can't get it all done? Thoughts swim in your head non-stop: Stuck in a mind-loop perpetuates an anxious ready state. No patience left, can't focus or center yourself. The key to re-balancing your state of being is ridding yourself of habitual self-torture and misery.

As an actress I learned to speak or yell out the inner dialogue of the character. Not repeating the words on the script's page, but capturing the inner dialogue going on in the character's head. Emotions would trigger and bam the character would come alive, a real person I could relate to and portray. The five senses cannot tell real from the imagined. And, we play mind games, consciously or unconsciously making life a drama, a sit=com, or tragedy.

To be real, enlivened in the NOW - release stress. Your inner dialogue needs to dump-out or it remains in a mind-loop. Physical exercise is a stress releaser: jogging, swimming, hitting tennis balls have beneficial effects. Ahh, but you keep missing the Gym? You're at your wits end, on deadline, car pooling kids. What to do?

Dump the Gunk 2-Minute Stress Buster

Indecent Exposure: "Two birds are mating outside my window, loud squawks and feather's flying." ml

If you're at home, alone preferably, close the windows so you don't disturb the neighbor's peace. Without thinking or editing,

♥ **Repeat OUT LOUD** what is going on in your mind. You might start pacing, even yelling, or crying. Keep speaking until there's nothing left in your mind, nothing left to rant.

♥ If necessary you can do the same exercise in the car; windows rolled up and you'll receive the same benefit. A good cry releases pent up emotions and gives space for a lighter energy to emerge.

♥ If you feel a surge of anger, put a pillow between your teeth to quiet the sound. Bite down on the pillow and release the feelings. Do it until it naturally quiets. In minutes you will feel a shift.

♥ Sit quietly and deep breathe for a couple of rounds. Allow a calm light energy to flow through you permeating every cell in your body. Allow the sweet energy to brighten your spirit.

Automatic Writing - Heals The Soul

"I am so spiritual and Awakened... I can't fall asleep."

From 8-years-old on I've purged, surged and self-merged by writing my innermost thoughts and feelings. My journals record life passages, and what bothered me, no longer has an affect. A stellar way to release stress and pent-up feelings. I've seen transformation, and lessons bop you on the head... when you write from the right side of your brain. The intuitive powerhouse, that Knows it all, what you've forgotten to be balanced and whole.

Automatic writing practice is done without thinking what you are going to write.

♥ Don't edit or judge. Let it flow.

♥ Start out just writing a thought or two or vent what you'd like to say to you boss and know better.

♥ You can also speak your thoughts OUTLOUD, as you jot down the essence of your experiences. When you've recorded the message for the day, you're good to go.

Fulfill your daily activities with a sense of calm. Your LightHeart is with you, an Oracle ever present, guiding you to contentment.

Reality or Not?

"I've got the answer, can you tell me the question?" ml

Do you assume that "your reality" is reality? What we contemplate is often pre-programmed by our past experiences and influences our concepts. Deep questions help us to Bounce out of our boxes and take off the blinders, the dark shades or rose-colored glasses. It's too painful, scary, or off-putting to look the underlying source of our locked-in beliefs. So we superimpose what goes on in our head, which is often unconscious. To cope we mock-up a virtual world... unaware we are the only one it. This 24/7 reality is ours alone, we are trekking through our daily adventures.

We Bounce into melding with others, feeling deep love, having fun, and sharing the ups and downs of life. Reality blockers show up as: irrational reactivity or lack of response, moments of feeling isolated, out of sorts, confused.

Most of us live in the boxes of our mind. We are conditioned by our parents, teachers, and society at large to believe the lies of who we are supposed to be. We learn to hate, to judge, to feel inadequate, or to assume we are better, smarter, dumber, or more just, than others of difference. The judgment boxes are tidily wrapped in gender, sexual preference, race, religion, or creed. We are taught to separate from the human family and to isolate in our limited views. Operating on automatic pilot we remain insecure, doubting our intuition.

By simply opening to the possibility "what we see could be unreal" - we can perceive beyond our rose colored glasses into the extraordinary. We see what others cannot see, a multi-dimensional world outside of our mind-loops, beyond comfort zones, and everyday ho-hum's. We discover an enlivened wonderment a place of creative living.

If your whole life is 'I' egotistically centered, or the other extreme, outwardly focused on minutia or global disaster, you may miss the bigger questions. "Who am I, why am I here, and what is my purpose? These timeless questions are so bantered about, like meaningless sound bites. AHA...take heed! They are profound and sublime queries and will lead you to 'who and what you truly are'.

Take Care Of Your Inner Child

Your Inner Child needs to feel safe, loved, and supported. When you are in a reactive mode, feeling out of sorts, often this is a histrionic trigger. You are reacting from a place of a 2-year-old, wanting your way Now. Or you're operating from your abused child that was neglected, abandoned, not listened to, and your feelings were squelched. "Children are to be quiet." "Leave me alone, you are such a brat." The message was 'be invisible, your opinion doesn't count'. Out of fear of being hurt, punished, or not pleasing our parents or care- givers, we learned to shut off our feelings. We squelched our creative impulses and denied our authentic and intuitive response.

Take notice of repetitive patterns of reactivity. Whatever is going on in your life, the issues that you are facing where you feel helpless, isolated, fearful of responding. Think back to when you first felt the feeling. You may have been 2-10-years-old, an adolescent or teen. What are the affects now? opportunity to make peace with reactive triggers and cultivate a caring relationship with the child within. Assure your little friend, who is 'forever' with you, that he or she is safe, loved, and nurtured.

Speak to your inner child, ask, "What do you need?" Listen and take charge. Simply say, "Go play, I'll handle 'it' and you will be OK." Practice when that familiar out of sorts childlike vulnerability nags - feel the instantaneous shift of clarity & calm.

Your inner child is longing for recognition. What is the young soul calling for? Nurturing, more fun, love? What is the child, adolescent, or teen's essence? Vulnerable, feisty, lonely? What qualities can you embrace, integrate, and merge with – allowing the childlike wonder, innocence, and magic to unfold?

Do We Have a Soul? Soul Proof?

"Did your make it to the Milky Way... while you were looking for your soul out there?" Train

UCLA did experiments as far back as the 70's... recording images around the moment of a person's death. A circle of cloudy smoky energy left the body...was that the soul, the infinite matrix of energy? Science itself is not exacting. I personally will not wait for that answer.

I feel connection with departed souls, who I know or sense...there is a holographic imprint of the person's essence. They remain imprinted in the hearts of those who love them and cherish their memory. No one can prove one way or the other. Nevertheless, over 60 million people in the United States alone have experienced unexplainable phenomena around loss of a loved one. Hearing voice, seeing an image or symbol, sensing an eerie message of the departed. I have a spiritual connection with my beloved son, it is healing and gives purpose to live life to the fullest. On my life journey I have assisted other people to connect with their loved ones. Tears, joy, relief, healing, and a sense of completion are a few of the Blessings they feel-n proof of our eternal soul.

CONNECT TO A DEPARTED LOVED ONE.

There's a simple process to explore, connecting with the spirit of loved one – igniting an eternal soul relationship that can be experienced NOW.

♥ In a quiet time, simply ask for a sign.

♥ Ask a question of your departed friend, family member, or someone you would have liked to have, but didn't.

♥ You may choose to write the question. And, without thinking ... allow the answer to flow through you on to the paper.

♥ Read what you have written and contemplate, what message you were given.

'

Beyond what we can see, taste, smell or hear. Beyond our analytical mind, we can learn to feel what others do not sense. In this multidimensional state... we are set free of the bondage of limited perceptions and perspective. We are set free, beyond the body and the mind to dwell in the field of infinite intelligence. To dwell in spirit everlasting.

CHAPTER 3

♥ WAY TO WORTHINESS...
...HEAL THE HURTS♥

"While they were healing my hurts...I was out partying." ml

Are you Self-Doubting or Fearful? Self-doubt is a human debilitating trait. Some of us experience it on a grander scale. For me the essence is to face the fear, determine the root cause, and choose whether to 'do it' anyway.

There is a timeless state of awareness; mediators, painters, joggers and musicians speak about...where you know you are not the doer. Action Flows through you without judgment or resistance. The freedom to BE transcends labels and judgments. When ling a label, CPA, Mom, Dad, teacher, dumb or smart, fat or skinny, becomes your identity core, you lose sight of your self worth and Being-ness.

You may blame working in a top-down fear-based environment or living with a nit-picky spouse as the cause of your low self-esteem. You spend your life either defending or

29

succumbing to abuse and thrashing. When we choose to accept our self with our frailties and assets, as a soul evolving, learning life lessons, we no longer live by other people's opinions of us. We give the battle of proving of our self-worth. Self worth and entitlement is an inside job...that flows outward, expressing our creative essence in all we say, think and do.

Enhancing Self-Worth

1. Give yourself permission to feel good... even if the project fails. You didn't fail.

2. Make a list - what are my strengths? What are my weaknesses? Don't edit. Personal and professional traits may intermingle. Now view your list. What is true? Are you too tough on your children, co-workers, or yourself? How can you soften your heart?

3. Are you covering up your mistakes and hiding, or do you acknowledge them and make corrections

4. Do you cringe when you're complimented? Do you ignore your accomplishments? If so, allow the compliment to exist, don't judge its value. Take it as face value. Allow joy to surface, similar to how a child feels when they put the last block on their masterpiece castle and it didn't tumble down.

5. Recognize both praise and blame come and go. The 'what' to count on is core essence of who you truly are.

6. Connect with timeless, infinite intelligence. Breathe and inhale deeply. Stay on the breath for a minute or two. From this space you will begin to sense your essence beyond what you say, think, or do.

7. Now for the fun. Pat yourself on the back, when you accomplish something. Smile when you've done a good deed. Hug yourself when you discover a mistake you've made. Acknowledge it and decide if, when, or how you choose to rectify it. And, remember you are your best friend, not a self-inflicted bully, sabotaging your good. *"I love myself, growing, knowing everything will be OK."*

Who Said This Is Who I Truly Am?

Who said I have to do all the things I am told? Who said this is true, real, and not a pack of lies? No blame of my parents, they did their best. No blame of the ignorance of greed-mongers, who have sold their souls to chasing hollow dreams. No blame, or shame, that I am the product of a society that has lost its way. So what to do? Let's continue to Reframe our reality, so each one of us can stand tall and proud to be 'who and what we truly are'.

Continue your truth-pursuit with Socratic questions; When you feel angry, miserable, fed up with life, or in a general quandary, ask yourself, *"What about that bothers me? What do I really want or need? Show me the way."* By simply asking your inner Knowing, unexpected answers shine a new perspective and often fuel the next question, readying you for right Action.

Reality Check: When your reality shifts, a newfound way of responding shows up in your behavior, with fewer over reactive or automatic responses. You sense what is Real. You create new life stories, viscerally. You respond with clarity, authenticity, and peace of mind.

7 Keys to Reframe Reality

1. **Spend time meditating,** and then contemplate what counts most to you.

2. **Whose voice are you listening to?** The worlds glib chatter throwing you off kilter. Or are you attuned in the Silence within your heart? Can you open to the sweet serenade of chirping birds? Or can you sing a happy tune, even though no one can hear you?

3. **Whenever you say 'they'** referring to a personal difference of gender, sexual preference, race, religion, creed...ask yourself *"Is that true or am I in my programmed box? Who told me that, how did I learn it?"*

4. Stop telling your life story and foibles, remaining in a loop chanting, *'This is my life now and forever."* List what is now and forever. Review the list, what is programmed, an untruth for you? Rewrite your story... and begin the improv' to live in newness.

5. Add daydreaming time...take moments to chill out. Feel, sense, and visualize exactly, in detail the life you want to live. Imagine the house, job, mate, travel, health and financial vitality. Allow yourself to see it NOW...living it. Watch how you uplift and how positive expectation trickles in surprise.

6. Spend time with friends, teachers, coaches who reflect the truth back to you. Who call you on your 'stuck stuff' and remind you to 'SHINE your good'. Surround yourself people you appreciate and return upbeat praise.

7. Allow your life to be your choice, don't' give it away for approval and acceptance. Honor your Uniqueness, special qualities.

A storyteller lives in our head, it exaggerates, creates emotional turmoil... If that doesn't work... it tells us of a beautiful world, filled with Love, hope, and happy times. Choose your best story... and Live it.

Bounce On The Milky Way?

Our emotional energy fields are combustible, miraculous, and similar to all energy in the Universe. This quantum discovery is an ongoing exploration in the scientific, spiritual, and alternative medical fields, which conclude: All energy is energy and cannot be destroyed, but it is agreed upon in these various approaches that it can be transmuted.

Transmutation of anger energy, for instance, occurs when you release it or blowout the energy. Blowing out energy fields allows us to up-tone our moods and emotions that hold toxic energy, preventing optimum health. Transmuting energy fields can be done through exercise, meditation, Qui-gong, yoga, swimming, jogging on the physical plane. You can then drop into a quiet neutral zone, which diffuses energy into peace and contentment.

From the perspective of the Milky Way....'gamma ray bubbles' extend 25,000 light years. Heated like the sun, the 'gamma ray bubbles' are twin lobes of cosmic energies that spiral inward, pulverizing, and compressing into intense magnetic fields. What happens to our whirling, swirling dervish energy as its light streams outward on its path? AHA... Bouncing thru the Milky Way? So crowded, soul dancers, vibrations enlivened, transmuted... from base metal (emotions, thoughts, beliefs) into gold (optimum potential).

Bounce Havoc Into Harmony

A black hole exists that is millions times larger than our sun, it has been located and is visible to us. Could it be that this hungry black hole is an intergalactic trash compactor gobbling up 'gamma ray bubbles' and other matter? In the same way our emotional energy trails are gobbled up into the similar black holes that extend beyond our bodies?

Every atom, every cell in our bodies are composed of the same particles in the universe. Every cell is a universe of its own, spinning and moving into homeostasis, or health or into disease. Between the cells are spaces that can be compared to the black holes in the cosmos. How would you like to discover how to move energy from inside out and diffuse your emotional energy and limitations? To maintain optimal functioning capacity of our bodies, mind, spirit.

Delete Bad Vibes...Amp Up Good Ones

Maybe you're feeling on top of the world and a phone call comes in from a downhearted friend. Their angst and frustration jolts your equilibrium. You feel stuck, compelled to listen and to bring them up while your good mood is dismantled, shredded into a downspin. Moods are contagious; we are hardwired to tune in to each other's emotion and allow empathetic response. Learning not to take on other people's emotions is having the awareness you are doing it. When your mood switches, say, *"This isn't my feeling. I am OK."*

Downer's Drain

"When you're feeling down and troubled...do me a favor...pretend I am out of town." ml

To reiterate, if you're confronted by a downer who is sad, irritable or in frenzy, pause and check in to see how you are feeling. If you are taking it on, remind yourself that this is not your state. Knowing how you feel gives you control and the option to continue the conversation or to delay it. Most importantly we want to avoid being the brunt of other people's moods. Complainers, complain. Blamers, blame. Victims whine and continue in a loop of misgivings.

Who told you being a whipping post for other people's whimsical feelings is being a friend? Boundaries are necessary to protect our sanity. Discrimination when to be available is the key. For instance, your teen is in a funk, upset over a friend leaving them out of an activity. Make time to listen without trying to fix them. Allowing their feelings to heard can lessen the hurt, confusion, or disappointment.

People ask me when I'm doing energy work with someone,

or running a HAHA Healers' session how I handle the unsettled energy fields? Do I pick up illness, or disease? Tuning into the universal energy frequency is a safe womb-like feeling. As the light frequency permeates, it does the healing, the unearthing of what needs to shift, and brings peace and resolve.

What comes through this field of awareness is amazing. It's like a puzzle that magically comes together. Fragmented parts of a person's psyche, physical, emotional bodies, as well as histrionic and ancestral causes can shift in moments. Illness, depression, and addictive behaviors can leave the person, and be deleted from their cognitive perceptions.

Finding balance with spiritual energy and physical energy is reconnecting the Chi, the life force. You can choose to commune with nature, make friends with your inner child, have fun, and allow creative juices to flow. Focusing on beauty.

So you stop to smell the roses...and a bee bites your nose. Lesson - mind your own business. So when a friend, co-worker or family member is in a bad mood, BE honest with yourself...tune in if you feel their vibes and take on the downer, it is your choice. If the exchange has left you bummed, remind yourself that you're not the source of the negative vibes, let them go and carry on your Merrie Way.

Wholly Connected- Heart Power

In order to BE whole (wholly) connected from the inside/out we must learn to wiretap what holds us back from resonating with our Heart Power...the magical place, where we are open to give and to receive LOVE.

Gradually opening up the recesses deep within...erupting, unresolved emotions could leave us wallowing in a vulnerable state. Exposing our weak side can fire-up past memories of being susceptible to hurt, abuse, or loneliness. In this defenseless and helpless quagmire, we want the longing, the pain, and the vulnerability to end. At our core, our tender heart is likened to a baby filled with a neediness to merge with someone else to help us feel safe and whole.

Satisfying the desire to be taken care of, loved, and nurtured while in this primal state of being can lead to bonding with someone, who is similar to our first caregivers, namely our parents. Most likely, they were incapable of being there for us – even if we know they did their best. If we allow transference to take place before unearthing and resolving core issues we are at risk of remaining stuck in a never-ending cycle, clinging to the familiar, perpetuating unhappiness.

Beyond Vulnerability... Contemplate

The following steps to begin the way back to wholeness and remaining open:

♥ It is important to recognize that your erupting debilitating feelings are temporal.

♥ Love cannot be replaced or taken away from you. Love is an infinitely intelligent emotion, an energy force that exists within you.

♥ Your child within is a teacher. Wholeness from a child's point of view is doing it all, expressing it in a natural creative way.

♥ When you feel yourself slipping into a defending state of being, turning off or hiding...IMAGINE what your creative child might choose to do. Go out on a limb for a moment, dive into the realm of possible alternatives...and Play there.

♥ Resonate Heart Power. Continue risking, opening to experience newness of authentic caring and receiving the same.

♥ Open yourself to whatever wants expression and create with it, BE it. You will learn to live in the lightness of Being, your birthright.

Connect, Breakthrough, Resolve

There are moments in life when the dots connect...and our

understanding is deepened. What once was an undercurrent of emotional turmoil, denial, or unknowing is released and we are set FREE.

Whatever is going on in your life now that is unresolved can be resolved. Part of shifting into resolution, is deleting the energetic pull the situation has on your psyche.

♥ Become aware of emotional triggers that create habitual reactivity.

♥ Check in with your body for Feedback. Feel the sensations that trigger pain, fear, and anger. Is it in your head, gut, heart?

Often before a breakthrough occurs you feel antsy inside, there is a knowing something unsuspected is about to occur, whether you are conscious of it or not. Or you may be breaking down, at your wit's end, not able to go on. Yes change is imminent; your spirit is calling out to you to listen, respond and grow...and to own your greatness in this life.

Spirit speaks to us in metaphors, we hear a story and relate. A bird flies overhead and we feel Free in the moment. A song plays and we harmoniously tune in. A friend or stranger says something and we grasp the deeper meaning. Our emotions speak to us, and we devour them, like hungry children to feel alive. Our emotional state of awareness connects body, mind, and spirit.

Breakthroughs occur when we give up the fight to keep things the way 'they have been'. Or to surrender our expectations of 'how things should be'. Holding on to resistance, unforeseen circumstance can disarm us, taking us by force, knocking us down. It may manifest as an illness, a great loss, or disappointment. With intention to change what doesn't serve our highest good, we can dissolve old patterns, limitations, stuckness, and erroneous beliefs. A perceivable shift in attitude can ignite new behavior and response. We feel REAL in the moment. We resonate Truth of BEing... accelerating our Knowing... our ONE with All.

Cynics VS. Lovers of Happiness

"Pat yourself on the back. We're here aren't WE?
If that isn't a Miracle, what is?" ml

Are you cynical or do you trek on optimism's path? Is Happiness your divine right or is it a random happening for the destined few? Glass half empty or half- full? AHA! Discrimination and seeing the downside, as well as the upside (in search of solution) brings a balanced approach to problem solving. Intuition combined with logic deals in the realms of Einstein's platitudes.

A God-given right - we breathe. That fares as optimism - not taking the breath of life for granted. Do you value the gift of life? If you are here, there is a bigger picture, a call you answered to incarnate at this time. The lucky sperm, the egg dropping at that moment is more than random chance - you chose this life, and your guardians of spirit are there to guide you.

Contemplate the notion of choosing your birth path, even it feels obscure or irrelevant. If you don't see the gift of life you will not value its potential. You will continue spinning in the illusion that an afterlife will have greater promise, or that there is nothing greater than you body or mind. Connecting with spirit, with the energetic life force, infinite intelligence is the way of flowing and knowing why you are here, why you answered the call.

I am a cynic in a sense: it starts inside my self - judgments or beating myself up for not fitting into the mold or agreeing with the herd. Qualifying my limited perspective, allows an opening, a creative expansiveness that inspires dreaming a wonderful and unexpected outcome.

Take a moment to breathe into the silence... Ask. 'What am I supposed to know or do today?' Listen, so you don't wake up and go into your routine. Ask your body what it needs, food, exercise, tender touch. Honor it. Listening to your inner voice, you are connecting to your authentic self. Often we feel like Swiss cheese with holes in us... we don't want to recognize the dark holes that linger in us. The neediness that exists deep within our heart.

HAHA HEALING

"The day you can laugh at yourself. You've arrived...whole & Fancy-Free."

Sandy, my dear friend was in the midst of chemotherapy and her life felt like an ongoing pity-party. On a ride home from the hospital she removed the cap concealing her hair loss. In the side view mirror she caught a glimpse of a shining baldhead with fuzzy hair spikes. She felt a tickle. "I looked like Jack Nicholson in the Shining. I began making odd and funny faces, laughing at myself in the mirror. A carload of teens pulled up next to me, and I continued with the antics. They began laughing with me. It was absurd, wonderful, and so freeing. I belly-laughed so hard I almost peed my pants." Sandy decided to carry laughter with her wherever she would go. A great healing practice, it sparks a twinkle in our soul.

Prejudice Hurts

Prejudice against another person or group of people can lead to isolationism and misunderstandings. Hate and angst fester, we close our hearts and remain locked in a box of erroneous beliefs. We may have been raised to be wary of people from a different ethnicity, religion, or creed. Our ancestry may have suffered in wars, or may have persecuted by a race of people. Holding these grievances can lead to violence in schools, the core of racism... to dominate or control other people.

Safety Net

♥ Hold your hands up in front of you, palms facing each other, about a foot apart. If you are right-handed, put all your fears and concerns into that hand. Lefties will focus on their left hand. Keep sending thoughts and energies of your fears and woes until your hand begins to feel heavier.

♥ Now focus your energy on the opposite hand. Looking at the palm, say aloud, "I am safe. Nothing can hurt me. All is well." Repeat it three times.

♥ Close your eyes for a few seconds, sense the calming your breath. Feel the shift in your body, mind, and spirit. You may feel lighter, clearer, at ease, balanced.

Practice the Safety Net until you own it as a daily habit. Calming your breath may even save your life one day.

Forgiveness

Forgiving is an anecdote for healing and gaining peace of mind. It is the Peacemaker's elixir, the ultimate answer to bullying, violence, repressed anger, prejudice. When you recognize that whatever happens to another person or group of people on this earth has an affect on you, and everyone else... you begin to see non-violence, loving one another as Truth of Being at Peace.

Compassion comes from an empathic heart connection that another's circumstance may be a breath away from our reality; in that understanding we know at our core...'There goes I'. Compassion reaches out to all sentient beings, to Mother Earth and to all of her creatures. It reaches into the depths of our soul...and we hunger for Peace in our hearts, in our relationships personal and with ALL. Whether we are conscious or not of our hunger for Peace internally or externally ... it exists as a natural way to be.

Hawaiian Forgiveness Prayer

Repeat the following words to make peace and dissolve lingering hurts.

Say person's name, *I am sorry for any pain I caused you. I forgive you for any pain you caused me. I forgive you. I forgive myself. Thank you.* (Repeat three times) End- *Amen!*

10 WAYS LAUGHTER HEALS

1. Commit to being light hearted. Lighten up is the advice my mother gave me when I became hyper and anxiety filled. It's an awareness that this is silly to be dwelling on whatever is bringing you down.

2. Feel appreciation and gratitude for what you have, instead of dwelling on what you don't have – or the fear of losing what you do have. That includes money, relationships, material processions, and loved ones.

3. Start or join a HAHA Laugh group. Watch funny videos. Tell jokes. Share funniest moments in your life.

4. Make up a funny story, take a real life issue that bugs you and find the irony, the satire, and get on a roll. Laughter jump-starts a bad, irritable mood.

5. Laughter is an exercise in itself. Your diaphragm and abdominal muscles are involved and your breathing is increased. Hearty laughs burn calories.

6. Burn out anger. You can't laugh and be angry at the same time. Tickle yourself or have someone tickle you to get that funny bone started.

7. Laughter is contagious. It attracts friends and makes sure you are good company.

8. Laughter is better than a placebo. It improves brain function, builds immunity and reduces the risks of ulcers, heart disease, and other ailments. Humor tones down the autonomic nervous system and helps the heart relax. It's the break needed to reduce pushing the body to the max.

9. Hang out with people who are fun. Skip the downers who want to see life as miserable, unfulfilling, and filled with gloom.

10. Bring humor into the bedroom- It amps up lovemaking and keeps a marriage spontaneous and fun.

Harmonious Communication

When you listen to the 'voice within' there is clarity, and you learn to Trust your inner guidance. Listening with your Heart brings contentment and intimate connection.

Listen, Speak Your Heart

♥ **Make eye contact with the speaker.**
♥ **See him as a friend, be curious about them. Allow a moment to expand beyond labels, beyond 'who' you believe they are.**
♥ **In that expansive awareness connect to their Being-ness. Who is it that is speaking or listening?**
♥ **Recognize the quality of your attention.**

So They're Sayin'

"I really can communicate...Only nobody listens. "

"No one understands me... It's tough being the only blond on the block."

"It wasn't really an argument...he just turned off his hearing aid."

"I've given up being right...as you know, I'm never wrong" ml

Sometimes we're wrapped up in what we want to say, we are not listening. It's a slight to the other person and we don't benefit by being in an anxious mode.

A glut of information rocket speeds from media hype, angry politicians, and disgruntled people slamming abusive slurs at one another. By separating a positive approach to life from the world's catastrophic state is not an either-or. Change is upon us and we can hear anger and frustration parroting in Media sound bites On the most personal level with our loved ones, co-workers and friends, our daily communication skills affect our relationships... denigrating or uplifting.

Facing fears and questioning internal motives brings honest inner-dialogue. How you self-talk, in your head, or what you say about yourself to others reflect your self-worth. Unless you're starring in a self deprecating Woody Allen film, self-put downs are sinfully disrespectful, surely not charming.

Respect for self and others creates positive communication and builds a strong ethical culture. Our children watch, listen, and model our behavior. Stop the 'no respect' brutality-lingo in our society. Shame on us if we don't show loving kindness to one another and wear a Smile to greet the day. Choosing positive attributes enhances positive activism and enlightened solutions for diverse points of view. Harmonious, heart centered dialogue goes beyond 'I'm right', 'You're wrong', embracing compassion.

Words are powerful. Each syllable contains a vibrational frequency. OM the primordial sound resonates with enlivened Stillness. When you chant OM your heart uplifts... and the mind quiets. Hold the Intent to uplift yourself and those around you...Choose Uplifting words.

HAHA Healing - LOVE

♥ Choose Uplifting Words – to change frequency.

LOVE   JOY   HAPPY   PEACE

♥ REPEAT Happy Words - over again in your mind or out loud. Within a minute or two... feel the uplifting shift.

♥ Pick these uplifting words, when in doubt, or when you feel anxious or sad. Turn gloom into joy.

Focusing on the breath helps to develop the habit of truly listening. Learn to slow down.

Hear the silence between your thoughts – this is where genius and the Improv' lives.

Gentlemen – A Soft Heart Reigns

Macho men, Groucho, and tough guys have one thing in common...they seem gruff and powerful. What is power to you? What is powerless? First off gentlemen, I will repeat... gentlemen. Is that an oxymoron? Certainly, NOT! In this greed-monger world we can no longer blame the patriarch – callousness is a human condition, beyond gender, race, or creed.

♥ **How can we turn on our heart-meter and establish the truth within?** How can we soften our hearts and reside, where authentic power reigns? **Contemplate** what you habitually say or do. Habits are reactive response, either diminishing spontaneity. What are you resisting or ignoring?

♥ **Take a moment and Breathe deeply.** Ask: "What dreams do I have on hold?" "What am I waiting for to bring me contentment?"

♥ **Music feeds the soul.** Singing, dancing, Mozart. Ah! Bounce out of the intellect; escape mind-babble battling your heart. The mind needs to dominate; to convince you it knows best. Who is it that listens to the mind?

♥ **Breathe again.** Connect with the ONE that knows it is not the mind. This is your true essence...your soft place of heart. Your true Power!

♥ **Walk Barefoot.** Connect with the vibration of Earth's heartbeat, a grounding stillness.

♥ **Take Time to connect with a loved one,** a friend. You don't have to take charge or know anything special. Discover, feel, see with your heart. Hear the silence between each word, between each breath.

This is the place of authentic power...a Soft Heart,

Gentle Men.

CHAPTER 4

♥ BE HAPPY WITH ♥

At a HAAH Healers session, we sat in the round with a group of Happy-Seekers pondering, "Why we choose to sing the blues? Fluttering outside a window, a humming bird danced in front of us... sending a message. We all laughed... imagining what it was saying, "Come outside and play." "Stop scratching your navel and dance." "It's creepy to waste your time." "Sing, really sing the blues, and watch how happy you are." What do you imagine the hummingbird is saying to YOU?

Busting Out of Chaos

Do you face the challenges, chaos, and trying times, or do you live in avoidance, procrastination, and hope it will go away? It's a choice to face a crisis head on, get past blaming and singing the blues. It's a choice to step-up; to BE the one you rely on and trust, to be a loyal friend to yourself. Inner strength is courageous, its efficient, and responsible. It doesn't forget a debt, or toss away a winning lotto ticket, or leave the tank on empty (auto or inner-you). You take care of biz' and fill up with joy.

When Life Implodes

Sometimes we are down, losing our grip on the Happy. When life implodes its an inward process, we feel the brunt of it. Our perception of the event or circumstance grabs us like a vice, squeezing out our life force. "I'm not enough", "Life sucks", "What's the purpose?" Imploding is a wake-up to examine 'what' is driving your life? You'll notice external stimuli and distractions no longer serve as a panacea to addiction, pain, loneliness, or boredom.

'What to do'? It's time to answer the call - Whether you call out to God, infinite wisdom, you intrinsically know that energetic vibrations are at work.

♥ Simply 'ask' what you want to manifest. "Show me the way to my good. I am open to feeling good, safe, and joyous."

♥ Your answer may show up as a symbol, a vision, or concrete answer. Trust intention's powerful frequency, materializing solution in the right place, with the right people, at the right time.

What's Your Happy?

"If my Happy is your misery. Then is your misery my Happy?" ml

I asked a friend, "What's your happy pill, so we could we bottle it?" He chuckled, "Happy = 99% living life as an adventure. The other 1% = Sweat the small stuff, later." Sweat the small stuff later, popped me in the belly. I had been sweating bullets over a lost suitcase...and I couldn't even remember half of the contents. Obviously, no item was really needed or couldn't be replaced. How about I should be grateful the plane landed safely? How about focusing on the Happy? Whoa! For me Happy is when I accept 'what is' and stop resisting 'what isn't'. Or... hanging out with 3-year-olds presents a new-mind-twister.

CHOOSE... uplifting creation, opportunity, contentment. Then misery takes a back row seat, anger melts away and hurts dissolve. When acceptance guides, we see with new eyes. Our inner world blossoms, renewal and rebirth. Life's internal and external metamorphosis resurrects a broken spirit and fills our heart with hope and magical design. Reflect on what thoughts are repetitive mind-loops. What beliefs do they hold for you? IMAGINE – how you would feel, by choosing an opposite belief? A new perspective... Maybe Chicken Little was gazing from the mountain top, and the sky wasn't falling down, after all.

Embrace Your Smiling Heart

♥ Find the place within...the quiet place. And remember someone who makes you Smile.

♥ Give a Smile freely...the returns are amazing. People open doors and welcome you.

♥ When you Smile from you Heart your eyes twinkle. Connect the two, with that awareness you will see what makes you twinkle. It shows up everywhere, in other people, for your delight.

♥ A Smile, a giggle, lightheartedness, will keep arguments away. You will learn to speak with tenderness, and slow down to overreacting.

♥ Smile to yourself before going to sleep...bring on a good rest and sweet dreams.

Love Bugs...Lover's of Life

Who would you describe as a Love Bug? Are you ONE? Love Bugs or Lovers of Life aren't seeking a saintly demeanor. An authenticity, a human touch of kindness resonates in their interactions with others. Becoming a Lover of Life begins inside, a swelling of the heart, a sweetness brings peace. Practice staying connected in word and deed. Relationships offer, a soothing, scintillating intimacy.

Love Bugs Daily Practice

♥ What brings you Joy: Miracles in nature, rolling rain clouds, babies crawling, and the morning dew. Practice joy connecting daily as a life habit.

♥ Choose to live life in the direction of Loving – choosing to follow 'what' brings a state of Harmony. Find the humor... Lighten your load.

♥ Radiate good feelings. Recognize the good in others. Compliment freely. Take in other's truth. BE sensitive to others.

♥ Risk, express true feelings. Reactivity, anger, judgments, shutting down is a daily testing ground. Emotions and feelings reside, and often preside over our behavior.

♥ Be aware when you are out of sync. Breathe into the moment.

Allow what is to BE!

Be A Lover Of Life...It's a Choice

"Five suitors are at banging my door. It's jammed, they can't get out." HA! ml

Observe when you put your self down, either in your head or spoken out loud. Just say, "Oops, not true". If someone else recriminates you...don't absorb the opinion. Leave the blame, shame, guilt where you find it...and move on with your integrity, inner Peace & Power. Put-downs are like rabid dogs in society. Let's stop badgering each other on bully pulpits. Can we boycott vicious media, slanderous outbursts, and politically charged hypocrisy? We the people are decent; it's time to model that strength of high-mindedness to our children – to live in Peace.

A light shines, a remembering of who we truly are...ignites in the space of heart stillness. Breathe deeply, no matter what, who, when, or where. Remember your voice within..."Love Life."

The "Real Me"

Imagine... Living the life you were born to live. Now what would that look like? Would you happier, kinder, loving, doing what you love. Would you dance, sing, fish, or bake brownies? What is REAL? True, existent, authentic, and the kicker... Real is not always seen with the naked eye. It has a multi-dimensional component, nurturing the muscle of transformation.

To BE Real... is an expansive way of being. It rejects past beliefs, hurts, disappoints, abuse - as a Geiger counter for healthy living. To honor authentic living - choose what you know is right for you, and commit to stand tall for YOU.

In these challenging times we're looking for rays of hope. It may seem dim because our focus is drawn to emotional upheaval. Changes may be happening so fast (job loss and personal crisis) we feel lost in the shuffle. As days pass quickly it seems that we have lost our way. What is happening to the "Real Me?" How can we get back to the unity with source, the spirit connection that guides our way.

Contemplate The Bright Side

Make a list of what brings on your happy, your contented state of being.

♥ What makes you smile, laugh, or feel good about yourself?

♥ What is your fondest memory? Who was in it, what were you doing, where were you?

♥ What do you love to do?

Make a list of the events, people, and situations that trigger emotions, and limited feelings of self. When reacting, and falling into a mind-loop of negativity... Pause, and acknowledge this is not my potential self. "I choose the bright side,

I choose the high road."

Since you were a baby everyone had an opinion of 'how you should be'. That included what you should say, think, or do. How can you look inside and discover your own truth when so many voices occupy your mind and juggle your heart? You can hold on to a thousand and one excuses, why you are stuck, wearing a fake mask, frozen heart, keeping love and your potential life in a freeze frame. Remember: Life is a moment-to-moment revelation.

Tap into your true essence by feeling your body's response. A twinge in the stomach signals fear of something. Butterflies indicate positive expectation. A rapid heartbeat can be the onset of anxiety. Tight shoulders, carrying burdens. Listening to your body's message identify how you feel, why you react, and ACT. I'm aware when I cringe inside, thinking, "Ah, maybe I shouldn't have said that." Either I uttered gossip about someone, acted like 'pleaser' instead of speaking up - and the result, it landed in my gut like a bomb. Be aware of fireworks going off inside of you. Ask the feeling or physical sensation, "What do I need to know that I don't see?" "What is this feeling, ache, or sensation, telling me?"

Know that you know! It's not a mystery, the 'Real Me' shows up ready to serve, when you choose to know! We are vibrational beings and our gut reaction alerts us, and zings anyone in our path. Our thoughts, words, and deeds are transmitted as energetic frequencies... kind or unkind. Every moment is an opportunity to express the highest, your truth in action. Everywhere you go you leave an energetic imprint. Can you douse resentments and blame, and uplift? It's a choice, every step, every word & deed. Choose.

Face Up...Be Authentic

"So if I'm the 'Funny Wise Woman', whose that grump staring back at me in the mirror?" ml

The Actor's Drama-Mask shows both the happy and sad face -- comedy and tragedy. We feel both of them and walk the razor's edge trying to balance the two extremes. Even if we think we're hiding our two faces, spewing emotional curveballs we all go naked in our truth. Hiding transparency of 'who you truly are? Masks are an inside job. They start with what we can't face about ourselves - the shame, anger, embarrassment, and pain we try to hide. What we cover-up are the lies we live with. Our internal shadows linger and haunt us. Unaware of duplicitous choices we make, our shadow self sabotages our authentic nature. We fail to discover what we love, what we truly care about, this arrested development diminishes our chance to live our potential.

We may show a phony face to the world. But who are we kidding, tricking, and who suffers the duality? You do. Yes, you can spend a lifetime uncomfortable in your own skin, or you can choose to risk breaking the chains that keep you bound.

Imagine taking off the false mask and standing naked in your vulnerability. How bad can that be? What is the worst that could happen? Are you afraid of showing your weakness that others will take advantage, hurt, reject, or abuse you?

If you answered 'yes' to any of the above, it's time to shift out of dread and apprehension and take charge. Waiting for life to be perfect leads to the perfect storm. Life will throw you a curve ball and charter a new course whether you choose it or not. Choose before a big pie lands in your face, or a gong hits you upside the head.

What's to hide, everyone you meet has something they're dealing with? Stripping down to what really matters, you diffuse haunting shadows and begin to actuate the life you were born to live.

Change Your Hat...Change Your Life

From an upside-down perspective... You ain't YOU.

Shout-Out! Mom, Dad, daughter, son, plumber, CPA, salesman, Yippes the list is endless. How about tossing your hats in the closet of no return, beyond limited concepts that define you? Here's what I did. I took negative "Who I am" labels and made a New-Me-Stew. Not talking rigidity here, I'm talking freedom.

Freewheeling…connected to loving nature and people. Loving what you do without having your little-ego-identity sewed up in it, slamming you at every turn to be more, do more. Telling lies, "You're not good enough, perfect enough, or deserving." So, are you ready to ignite fiery, creative potential …the seeds of genius try my recipe below.

Toss Labels In A Big Pot

♥ Envision all your preconceive notions, "I'm not a good mom or dad" "I'm too old to learn" "Once a beauty queen, always a beauty queen."

♥ Boil those lies up…to puree; until the blend is so tasty, you are REAL… Loving your Happy Stew.

Face up to your greatness without apology or justification. Perform acts of kindness for yourself. Treat yourself with respect, gentleness, Love. Treat yourself as your best friend. Have compassion, laugh at yourself, have fun. This is the key to discovering self-love. This is the reason for your existence, your true nature…To Be that Love and spread it to all you meet.

Improv' Shifting Gears

"Hey gorgeous Hot-Mama. I turned around to see who they were talking to. Da! There was no one there but ME. Flattery goes a long way, tingles a Happy."

REAL is not 'what' you are doing, it's 'who' IS doing it. When I'm working with my accountant, I'm more left-brain concentration. When I'm filming "MerrieWay Day, I'm a right-brainer, bringing on the funnies. Hopefully you'll agree, or not. See that's the biggee, letting go of the result, the need for approval, being on top. That doesn't mean you're not on top of your game, you just don't need it to be whole. To be YOU...the one inside that bubbles up with joy, the one that has compassion for yourself, as well as for others, is the Knower-- Infinite wisdom.

Our brothers and sisters globally have suffered climatic, wars, and inconceivable devastation. We empathetically feel their pain, anguish, and fear. Out of this recognition, it is evident how hopelessness can set in. Praying for answers to understand our plight as humans, the suffering, and such great loss... five powerful words were given to me, **"I AM A LIGHT BEING."**

I AM is the essence of spirit...for each ONE and ALL of us. "I Am A Light Being." Repeating this affirmation will ignite the freedom that exists beyond the body and mind. Knowing your soul is connected to every other soul on this planet is a liberation from the illusion of being separate. You can connect beyond the things that you see. In the awareness that you are a multi-dimensional being, you perceive, and see what others do not see.

In the higher vibrational frequencies, ascended Masters, our guides, send messages loud and clear, directing Light Forces to make changes in our DNA, to Flow in an expansion of consciousness. We are spiraling into self-realization, and the recognition that collectively we are ONE consciousness. We breathe the same air and feel the human condition as ONE.

It is our birthright to know there is a reason for all that appears REAL, the movement of Chaos that can devastate and the Eternal Light that fuels the Flame of Truth. The Is-ness, whatever is occurring is this expansion. Awareness is the Wake-Up call to operate from authenticity... To drop resistance, limited beliefs and to become ONE with IT, ONE with all sentient Beings...LIVING the One-ness of I AM.

Repeat: "I AM A Light Being" three times. Breathe deeply, with intention as you say the words. Feel the expansiveness and the joy that permeates through every cell in your body. Feel the presence of the I AM...the God within and the God that is omnipresent...as YOU!

Maybe we've been here before, another lifetime, another planet. Or maybe we're all swimming in a fish bowl, and we perceive it as the universe. Maybe?…Maybe…Maybe!. All of that doesn't matter: BE HERE NOW is the only moment that counts. Can you toss 'ego hats' in the closet of no return? Which label bothers you the most? Come on fess up. OK, I will. One label's a keeper. no one can take away, "I Am LOVE."

TANTRA… Pleasure & Intimacy

"Come on baby light my fire" "I'll take you higher"

What do these lyrics have in common with Tantric Yoga, the ancient practice of deep breathing, movement, and connecting the 7 chakras or major energy fields in the body? AHA the practice has many health benefits, multiple orgasms is one, and often lasting for hour or longer. Oxycotin, the pleasure hormone kicks in and "Will take you higher" and most certainly, "Light your fire."

Movement from the base of the spine, known as the root chakra, releases a fiery red ball of energy that can engage the second chakra, in the pelvic area, the sexual energy zone. When this powerful energy field ignites, it can move upward, to the other six chakras, the belly fire (emotion & control center, heart (intimacy & Love), throat (communication), third eye (intuition) and finally to the top of the head...a connecting to the Source of all

Knowing and Creation.

Tantric Yoga requires discipline, benefits include, sexual blissful union, healing the immune system, activating the pituitary gland, connecting to source of wisdom, the magical trump card.

Sacred Woman

Sacred Woman, oh great goddess, Mother Mary, Gaia, all exist for our pleasure, to remove the pain, doubt, and all interference with Truth. It is time for us to gather the wisdom of the ages and model it. This is for the sake of our children, for Mother Earth, and all her creatures.

The men are waiting for our return. They are our devoted husbands, sons, brothers, nephews, grandfathers, friends and lovers, who too have forgotten. To wake up the masculine they need our nurturing; our Mother Earth strength and KNOWING. The male, the protector, the One that adores his woman, wants her back. His heart calls out for her, and her heart needs his touch for balance and Harmony.

Don't back away and retreat to a practical comfort zone. Go beyond limited vision, and discover the magic existing in realms of the unseen. The essence of Woman is lightheartedness. She brings in the dawn, illuminates the sunlight, nurturing and brightening the hearts of every one she meets. Her spirit expands throughout the universe, and we can hear her voice in thunder, feel her presence in the wind. She is everywhere, in everyone, everything, animate and inanimate.

Sacred woman knows her feminine power. Deep in her core she is authentic, whether good, bad, sexual, or ugly. She is visible, magnetic, and unafraid to express her authentic needs, and to release what doesn't serve her, or humanity. Standing tall, evolving in her potential self, guiding the future, knowing all is OK.

YOU Are Born Of Woman... You Are Sacred.

- ♥ Begin each day with that Knowing.
- ♥ Breathe it with every breath, walk it every step.
- ♥ Inhale the strength of LightHeart belonging,
- ♥ BE, Live as Sacred Woman, You are ALL THAT.
- ♥ No one can stop you - you live your power.

SoulPods

Great friends can make you cry. Yes! You laugh so hard you're brought to tears.

A Soul Connection is eternal. You may feel infinite connectors, your SoulPods...swimming with you in your vibratory field for a lifetime. SoulPods are those people, animals, dream-beings, spiritual guides that you feel at home with. You recognize how comfortable you are with them. You can sense another's presence, no matter how far or near the physical distance. You can tune-in to them and feel peace, calm, and joy of connecting.

You may have dreams of someone, you have never met. In the quantum energy field, in the actuarial multidimensional world of spirit they are ever close, helping you to cope at various times in your life, even teaching you in your dreams to understand aspects of your life, to make changes, to gain a new perspective.

No one can make changes for you. No One can tell you your truth. You must decide your destiny, moment by moment. We must learn to be strong, to discriminate the bombardment of daily influences, the input off media, parents, peers, global frenzy, to loving gestures. We are put here on this earth to handle the challenges before us and to learn the lessons. We won't learn if we don't risk stretching our concepts, our limited vision, and our ego-state that wants to be right and crush all obstacles in its way... of controlling our limited perspective.

To BE... is a state of connecting to infinite wisdom and light. The space where genius lives, the space of quantum possibility. BEing is who we are at our core. A place of all knowing...fluid, everlasting, transmuting resistance. To BE in this state of wonder, a REAL authenticity emanates in our thoughts, words, and actions. We don't need to lie, to hide, to pretend all is OK, when it isn't. Or to cry wolf to get attention, or act-out as a victim. Denial is no longer a choice... because we choose to live in recognition of 'what is'.

Take time to BE... to Breathe in the light of Being...Breathe with an Awareness of this infinite soul connection...the thread of spirit to this human life. When we falter, we can simply choose to recoup. We Pause, Listen to the Voice within. In this space we up-tone our spirit, we become more lighthearted, and we LAUGH. Laughter is a soul connector, a toxic release and healing valve connecting with innocence, wonder, the magic of Being. In this magic we can accept our self, and love our self for who we truly are. Masks dissolve, we smile, celebrate life, and have gratitude for our breath of life. This LOVE is expansive , eternal, and takes on many forms. It is unconditional, compassionate, and kind...We connect with other souls, in Love, as Love, for the sake of Love ...sensually and eternally.

Soul Mates

Our first juicy moment together, I loved the icing, you loved the cake...

Ahh. Are you seeking a Soul Mate, a life partner to share your life? Or are you in a wonderful relationship? Maybe you're settling in an abusive situation, or in a marriage that has dissolved into the Grey Zone. Remember: the #1 relationship begins with you - how you treat yourself, your commitment to honor, respect and love yourself. You will attract what you feel worth of having. As you express your needs, no longer settling for abusive, or toxic relationships, a shift occurs in who you attract, choose to be with, and how you choose to be with them. A dynamic frequency is set in motion for magnetizing heartfelt intimacy.

In the same way you are growing, unearthing your limitations your partner must be willing to the same. You cannot do soul work for anyone else or change them into what you desire or need. No matter what the sizzle or attraction is initially without the component of mutual respect for each other, and finding true friendship, and mutual values, the sizzle will wear off. Your differences, annoyances, grievance glaring on center stage. Soulmates work it out, heart to heart to rekindle the spark.

After twenty-five years of marriage Leslie and Ron related how they maintained a juicy-loving relationship. Leslie beamed, "Ron always has my back. He's there supporting my kudos, or comforting me at my beside during a major surgery. He doesn't resent giving, he's a generous lover, and I feel emotionally safe."

Ron said , "Leslie is the smartest woman I know, I appreciate her. We're both headstrong, so we commit to speak and listen to each other from the heart. We never to go to bed angry or in a huff. We talk about it, so we don't let hurt feelings linger, even if we disagree. No competition, we support each other's passions and dreams. She's my lover, companion, my great teacher."

Contemplate and write down the qualities most important to you in a mate.

Such As, kindness, lighthearted, sense of humor, likes to have fun, caring, willing to have an open heart, grounded is similar values, ability to forgive, curiosity to learn something new, be willing to look at shadow and limitations, to communicate from heart. Is pursing their life purpose, financial contributor, spiritual seeker. Your list may differ, or have some of the same tenets.

Hold your vision for a great relationship. Recognize what you want and don't settle. In relationship... agree that Love is your guidepost. Choose to help one another to rise above your small egos. Swiftly move through a disagreement, allow space to recoup. No longer alone, you can count on each other, be lovers and friends, make mistakes, talk about it, and be authentically human. You can trust, be vulnerable, expanding open hearts, operating out of divine guidance. Sound too perfect? Contemplate why? If you choose to dwell on your miserable past, that is what you will recreate. No need... finding a Soulmate is possible.

> Make a LOVE Intention: "I Love myself." "I am open to Love." "I am Love." I live in Love." **Or create your own intent.** Write it down. Carry it with you. Keep it visible. Repeat it out loud or silently several times a day. Repeat it 11 times like a mantra, when you feel down – ease into that Peace of Love.

LOVE ACRONYM

L – LIGHT

O – OPENS

V – VISION

E – ETERNALLY ENRAPTURED

Love Yourself... LOVE, LOVE, LOVE.

CHAPTER 5

♥LIVING THE IMPROV'...
...GO WITH THE FLOW♥

"Improv' = Lightness of Being, it requires your intention to be present each moment, immersed in the NOW." ml

I was up at the crack of dawn for a conference call...I could hear a nest of baby birds chirping. Breaking all formality I put the team on the speaker to hear the sweet love song. Our meeting took on a lighter note and it went so smoothly. The lesson was to Breakout of the crusty mold of 'how' to do something and embrace life's gifts.

Thoughts and sensations can be uplifted with intentional awareness. That same day, I watched the piles of work...shrink into completion. Why so fast? When you love what you do...time slips away and joy fills the moment. Pick that 'something you love' and do it. An ongoing choice to seek out what we love. And most importantly, it starts inside by loving yourself.

Volumes written and spoken by wise ones lands on deaf ears, unless we take action. Hearing and feeling what's beneficial can evoke a calm state. To duplicate that calm in our outer world, we incorporate our actions in a concretized way, so our outer life begins to match our inner state. Synchronicity of events occurs. We accept what is going on…and gently make changes in alignment with our life's calling…we burn our Karma on the road to Loving Life.

What is stopping you? Are you waiting for your life to take-off? We make excuses waiting for the moment, the demarcation point that will lead us to our purpose, our happiness, or worldly success. So we compare ourselves with other people.

We believe people with worldly fame, power, and fortune, have found the key to happiness. Comparisons lead to feeling despondent, unworthy, or even hopeless. We can only know our inner state - not any one else's. We must have compassion for our self, honor and respect our self…before we can genuinely experience compassion for others. And elevate to 'There goes I.

Claim Your Extraordinary Birthright

The belief our ideal life will begin at a future time is a lie. What is true? Life is precious it's a gift you possess right NOW.

Focus on what the treasures you have. Focus on the breath, one breath at a time…your connection to life force. When you are present in this moment whatever pain, hurt, disappointment or misunderstanding you have...can shift by having gratitude. Simply ask the part of you that is the all knowing One...to guide you. Keep asking for guidance.

Still the mind with breathing and trust you will find what you have always known is there. You have been too busy looking outside of yourself to see. Ask, see, and live your truth. No one else can tell you what is right for you. For me I Remember..."Love is in the Air...Breathe".

Comfortable In Your Own Skin?

"About ageing... I decided not to sign up." ml

Are you comfortable in your own skin? Happiness is not a quest, it's a state of mind and that doesn't mean that you're Pollyanna if you see the glass as full. But, if you are uncomfortable within yourself, no matter how successful you are in this life, there will be a hole in the core of your being that needs to be filled. And so begins the quest for Happiness: Learning to live in harmony brings contentment, and happiness is a by-product. We deal with our pain, we admit to our addictive behavior, and we can transform into enjoying a lightness of being.

As a comedienne I have had the joy of giggling. You can't worry or be miserable when you laugh. You feel lighter and you might even feel happy. This isn't superficial, it's a gateway to heal and be healthy in mind and spirit. Call me Pollyanna, I prefer to say "I feel wonderful" and act as if, rather than dumping every miserable feeling I have on the world. Acting as if is also a transformational device that forms new ways of being OK with what is... I choose Happy.

Your Talent Lies In Your Choice

Stella Adler, the grand dame of the Russian theatre taught me a life lesson, 'Your talent lies in the choices you make.' If you keep choosing, the same-old, going upstream against the current the results often bring disappointment. Over efforting, pushing for what we desire, high expectations of how things should turn out, are burnout stressors. Using the wisdom of the Improv', develop your intuitive muscle, trust it, and receive the goodies as they arrive. In God's time. Choose to risk, to shift, spin on a dime, be flexible, and malleable. Choose to say 'Yes" to your good, that's real talent manifesting... in action.

TV Stars & Soap Dishes

Aside from starring in over 35 TV/films, during the famed

Luke (Tony Geary) and Laura (Genie Francis) wedding, 30+million people watched us and Liz Taylor. General Hospital skyrocketed and was Ranked #1 soap, an all time phenomenon.

College students were avid fans and I appeared in forums across the nation, including a fiery symposium at Harvard. There were after work parties, at local restaurants and pubs where General Hospital was taped and viewed over and over. Discussions prevailed about the cliffhangers and what would happen next. As to the impact the Soap Opera genre had and still has on society the diehard fans and occasion viewers debated and reflected on the influence, the inner workings of family, deceit, corruption, love-triangles and the like.

I was a working girl, getting to the set everyday having a ball, doing the funnies for 12 hours at a pop, and we shot 100 pages a day. I was apoplectic the first day I was in over 70 pages. Anna Lee, an old timer comforted, "Don't worry honey we all go home at night. Whew a relief. In 4-inch stilettos, that's dedication.

TRIVIA: Merrie Lynn is an improvisational actor -Robin Williams performed in the same improv' group.

Creative Jumpstart

Nothing is going right - Your brain rattles non-sequesters, "Maybe it's this?" "What about that?" Reeling on overload, no fresh ideas or solutions to dilemmas are forthcoming. You blame your seeming failure on the thrashed economy, your screaming kids, your divorce, burnout.

Further warping rational perception you cleverly make-up excuses, more excuses, even more. You're convinced this happiness stuff is pile of bunk...if you can't sell it, it ain't coming cheap. Filled with combustible energy...you send out a soul call resounding across the universes. Sleepy giants awaken, Goddesses gather, Saints and the like are watching... as your Muse magically appears.

Lure the Muse - Inspiration Waiting

Our Muse is an all knowing' source – a well of truth, joy, a juicy reservoir springing fresh ideas, answers to quandaries. As a magical genie mysterious and profound - it's born in stillness, where great Saints, inventors, artists, and truth-tellers live, sing and dance. Most simply, it's the essence of the self; the creative space within, connected as 'One' to all there is, was, and ever will be.

♥ To release your entrenched mind-spin - take a 10-minute break from habitual stress-brain rattling.

♥ To get the frustration, anger, and poor-me syndrome out of your system - allow a two-minute rant. Time it, any longer is a no-no. Go-ahead full-blast blame, shame, tame!

♥ Run in step, jog, swim, and bring up the breathing.

Live the Improv'... Go With the Flow

1. **Childlike Wonder** – Approach each day...with a beginner's mind and heart. Anticipate the best with positive anticipation. Know what you can change. Do it. Know what you can't change and surrender to that 'ism'. What is...IS... releases resistance.

2. Take risks. Life is about not having answers. Taking chances and risks. Make the most of every moment, all without knowing what is going to happen next.

3. Be your own best friend. It is easy to blame and shame yourself, but now is the time you deserve the most love and kindness of all.

4. Every day is a new beginning. Risk new ventures. No guarantees, we don't know what's around the corner. You'll be in flow...finding that new route, new experience. So get off you butt and venture out to see.

5. Big deal so you fall down Flat? Come up with a smiling face. Making mistakes is part of learning. Get the lesson and move on.

6. Live everyday to the fullest. Appreciate every moment, as if will be your last.

7. Lead with your heart instead of your head. When you come from your heart you come to your senses!

8. Meditate. Take time to just smell the roses. Breathe into your core. "Be still and know that you are God" With that Knowing... your Life Purpose will be revealed.

9. Drop the melodrama, the serious mind-set. Bring on the humor; drop the 'I have to know everything.' Adult doesn't mean serious, no fun in life. Enjoy, expand, and giggle.

10. Take a 'Me' vacation. Do something for someone else. Give 22 Smiles and Hugs...everyday. Guess who gets the goodies...it's a two-way joy ride.

What Say You?

I love the saying, *"A smile is the shortest distance between friends."* I'd add a hug too. Being a comedy actress I was paid to giggle up the fun. It spilled over into my life as lightheartedness. It is a choice to choose joy and remember - both tears and laughter are stress releasers and healing. Truly a smile is a definite precursor to a giggle. Find the things that make you smile, and guaranteed, 'Life smiles on those, who smile back'.

I believe it was Billy Crystal who delineated the difference between the class clown and the class comedian. "Class clown is the one who runs across the football field naked at halftime, and the class comedian is the one who talked him into it. Seems the jumper is the clown and the dare maker is the comedian."

Laughter... Overwhelm Buster

"If paradise is a quiet mind, hell must be my neighbor's dog barking." ml

Busy, Busy, Busy. Hurry- up! Deadlines mounting, to-do-lists. Overload and overwhelm, cramming it all into one stress-filled day. What is a day? Imagine we are sitting in the round...answering that question. Most simply, it's a 24/7 agreed upon standard measured by the rising and setting of the sun. Within that natural ebb and flow - birds chirp at dawn, butterflies fly in the sunlight, and owls hoot through the night. It is in this stillness of BEing; a sweetness of harmony resides. Harmony by definition is an agreement, an accord, and synchronization. The opposite is friction, dissension conflict. If we are in harmony with our true nature, stress cannot co-exist.

Laughter is an energetic harmonic, a flowing state of being. It raises our happiness trigger (releases hormones) in the brain and kicks in a relaxed response. Laughing is fun and it flushes out stress. I've had moments laughing so hard I cried. And, even snorted, I admit. These are precious moments – that are often precipitated by silliness, irony, a slapstick guffaw.

Think Funny – Learn to Spot Funny

Gander at Grandma's teeth in a glass. A grasshopper landing on your head. Even a little smile can change a stress-filled moment. It's an instant shift- a reprieve from agitation and disharmony. Humor is a proven anecdote to pain. It's a healing agent that diffuses stress, anger, frustration, and misunderstanding. Emma's 'giggle' spilled into my daily, making me appreciative of its power... to live a healthier, happy life.

Merrie Lynn Muses: Want a motivational burst of energy? Laughter is the ticket.

Knowing you Love IT – Brings On Passion & Joy

"It was love at first sight...we went for a walk and he brought his leash." ml

There are joy signs everywhere. Warm friends tickle your heart, a sunset shines the gift of a good day's end, a fresh breath of air enlivens your spirit. So why do we ponder on the negatives, only choosing to see dark stormy clouds? Exhaustive habits lurk as a cornerstone for staying stuck. To be free and to live in joy...can begin by looking at the pair of opposites that occur within our psyche. And switch to positive. When feeling lack *Repeat: "I am blessed with all I need."*

The power and strength of the opposites...pain and joy, resentment and forgiveness, fear and freedom, amenity and Love, to name a few, enliven and help us know why we are here, why we are living our life. Our purpose is revealed when we feel, see, and acknowledge the extraordinary nature of life's possibility. We bail out riding an emotional roller coaster. We release pent-up feelings; we balance a peaceful estate of mind, and rest in a harmony. The highs and lows reach a neutral zone...the place of equanimity.

Know You Love It…simply means to choose what makes you feel good, what brings joy into your life. Passion and purpose ignite from knowing. What you don't like also signals what to pursue. Maybe you don't like skiing anymore, or life's repetition.

Make a list of what you enjoy doing, from work, hobbies, to socializing. Feel the power in just thinking about it. Make a list of what you don't enjoy, maybe you are fed-up with the inequities of the homeless. This too can be a motivator, a passion to become pro-active. Review both lists and contemplate revelations.

♥ **Do you need to measure how joyful you are**? Do you need to compare your state of being with other people? Do you need to jump for joy to know it exists?

♥ For one day practice the art of balance...when you feel remorse, hate, judgment, hurt, or pain...allow it, without resistance. In allowing, we don't expend energy to change it.

♥ Observe your emotions...as if watching a melodrama. Allow it to shift into a romantic comedy or a sit-com. When you drop the need to be sooooo dang serious...watch how you laugh at the silly's and have a ball.

♥ Joy isn't attained by focusing on what we wish to have. Trying to fill cravings is a bottomless pit, frustrating and unfulfilling. Consumed by what's missing becomes the goal, and we remain unaware of beauty in the moment. Knowing what brings joy is an internal switch, accepting and flowing.

Bring On A Smile... Turn On The Joy Switch

1. Watch what you crave from the aspect that is OK to have it and OK not to have it. A calm, gentle peace can bubble from inside and make our daily experiences more joyful.

2. Catch yourself comparing what others have that you don't. Appearances are often a misperception, a deception that leaves you unhappy.

HAHA's Blow Out The Feeling

Don't **'Repress...Express.'** When feeling uptight, angered about something, or feeling anxious. Not to disturb anyone use a pillow to muffle sound.

♥ Hold a pillow. Put the pillow's edge between your teeth.

♥ Gently bite down. Do not clench your jaw or bite down hard on your teeth.

♥ Release the pent-up feelings with sounds, a yell, or cry out. Release for one minute.

♥ How do you feel? The issue may have dissolved into a lighter feeling. If you have a residue of feelings - Repeat the energy blow-out for another minute or two.

♥ Pat yourself on the back for 'Expressing instead of Repressing'.

♥ Go about your day. Take a walk, jog swim, if you can. Or continue your tasks at hand.

Lead With Heart and Intuition

How can we sustain our real passion for full-blast living and not be squelched by resistance? Let's examine 'to do it or not do it'? Issues may entail starting a new biz or relationship, dissolving the old and creating a fresh start, or even moving to a new location.

♥ Focus on the issue at hand? What are you afraid of, concerned about?

♥ What is the upside and the downside?

♥ Yes, No, Yes? Undecided, pause. Ask, "Is this right for me now?" Allow your body to answer. Feel uplifted, or a drop in energy? Trudge past fear, get your toes wet, take first step. YES!

Daily Practice: Reflect on what IS happening, changing, or what you're resisting.

♥ Do you source what's meaningful from within? What is your core/purpose and priority, what is your commitment to it?

♥ Are you procrastinating? In what areas, financial, love relationships, not cleaning up the kitchen? What we avoid needs our attention, needs to be handled. It's a growth lesson. Just doing 'it' releases a stuck energy field for expansion.

Choosing to step up for growth is #! Clarity of purpose takes hold and you are propelled into amazing synchronistic happenings.

Invoking Intuition – Developing the Skill

♥ Be mindful of physical setting. Indoors: select soothing music, scented candles. Outdoors: light a bonfire, gaze at rolling clouds, listen to a babbling brook. Invite new insight to reveal core truth.

♥ Clear your mind: Deep breathe for two minutes to gain clarity on your query: a situation, relationship, or direction to take. Ask questions like, "What do I know?" "What can I do? "What else do I need to know?" Allow your intuition to surface, with a feeling, sensation, image.

♥ Gauge whether you feel light or heavy inside. Lightness: a YES possibility. Heaviness: pause, before moving forward.

♥ Inner Physician: Close your eyes. Tune into your body. Do a mental scan from head to toe. Visualize each organ. Let the organ or body part speak to you. If it's not feeling healthy, ask why? Send positive, loving, healing energy to that part of the body.

♥ If you feel queasy, chilled, or nauseous around someone or when thinking of a situation, listen to your body. It could be a warning. Stay aware.

♥ Practice:
  • Ask someone to give you the name of a person you don't know and describe him or her. Don't think. Just do it.
  • For Mastermind guidance – Dialogue with Intuition.

Trust inner Knowing … Don't squelch your innate gift.

Anti-Aging Secret...Smile, Laugh, Giggle

"You can't smile and worry at the same time"

On the first day on a TV set- the director came over to me and held a mirror up to my face. He didn't say a word. I looked at him. He looked away. I giggled a bit nervously and glanced into the mirror. I frowned wondering, "Maybe he doesn't like me." With that thought my face squished into a mass of wrinkles.

"Gotcha", he laughed. "Take your pick, while you're young. Smile or frown. Smiling keeps you young. Frowns follow you forever."

I thought about what he said, after all we were doing a sit-com – everyone including the crew cracked up all day. The funnies were among us.

Shortly thereafter I stopped by my friend's real estate office. As I went down the aisle toward his office I noticed big standup mirrors on each desk. One of the sales agents was intensely chatting on the phone. She paused, obviously listening to the person on the other end of the line. Intentionally sitting up straight she glared at herself in the mirror, and flashed a fake smile, baring her teeth she widened the grin, until it blossomed into a happy smile. Her demeanor shifted, she lightened up her intensity.. and began speaking in a friendly tone.

I was intrigued thinking, "What is this group up to? Beverly Hills anti-aging?" Not exactly, I found out were practicing a sales technique that helped them deal with their clients in a more friendly way. Smiling into the mirror helped to ease the stress of selling and to insure a welcoming tone.

Lucky for me I smile a lot. I laugh and giggle and belly a guffaw.

Merrie Lynn Muses – Go for that big Smile. Grin. Bigger, show those pearly whites. Let that smile blossom into happiness. Put a smile on your face and greet the day. Pass your smile to everyone you meet -- a friend, a stranger, your lover, your child. You'll get more compliments than you can imagine. The world smiles back at you.

In the words of Dr. Seuss, "Fun is good."
How y'all, doing, what's up with your funnies?

As we continue down the path of raising ourselves, and raising our kids... Let's put joy and laughter in the mix. As daytime's first comedienne, and frolicking on 35 TV/Films...many of them comedies, I learned... not one soul on the planet wants to hear gripes, preaching, complainers, and blamers. The bitches and got a lot of hate mail. But those of us, who made viewers laugh until they peed their pants, were forgiven our foibles. Let's go for...Laughter is great for body, mind and soul. Spontaneously enjoy and relate to each other. Whether you play charades, paint the fence together, or watch "I Love Lucy" reruns...you're on a happy trail.

MerrieWay Recipe 4 a Happy Day

♥ AHA! There is a reason to be Happy: It is your birthright, a natural way of being.

♥ SMILE 22 times: At someone, yourself, funny movie. The shortest distance between two friends is a Smile.

♥ Give 22 HUGS: A ♥ to ♥ connector with someone includes you, pets, a teddy bear.

♥ Be PLAYFUL: Sing a happy tune. Skip, bounce, blow bubble gum.

♥ Be an OPTIMIST. Give 22 COMPLIMENTS. Acknowledge yourself, too.

♥ Share or send your HAPPY THOUGHTS or words with others. Show expressions of GRATITUDE through prayer, words, and acts of kindness.

♥ Go gentle with yourself and others. Delicate is rare in this upturn world.

CHAPTER 6

♥LIFE AS AN IMPROV'
IT IS, YA' KNOW!♥

I'm convinced that Life is an Improv. If it weren't you would be born with a script in your hand. In the Play of Life, the actor is you. By exploring acting techniques, we can expand our capacity to flow freely, to feel empowered and play in spontaneous creativity. I love being a clown – a comedy gal. I can do the unspeakable, say the unthinkable. I can laugh through the pain, strife, and nonsense in life. I can belly laugh through tears and release all the tension, misery, and angst from my soul. I grab a giggle, a sparkle, and a teasing glow. I stay young. I laugh a lot.

Lucky me! I was in an improvisational (Improv) comedy group run by Howard "Howie" Storm, the director of the sitcom Mork & Mindy. Cindy Williams from Laverne and Shirley, Fred Grandy (Love Boat), and Teri Garr (Tootsie) were in the group. Howie's innate ability not to go for the joke and let the funny happen, allowed him to be the most viable director for Robin

Williams, who played Mork, an alien visitor to earth. Howie let Robin fly, knowing moments before a taping that Robin would land on the mark with the most brilliant choices. He didn't control Robin's comedy genius. Instead, he had the uncanny ability to harness it and capture it as it went down.

Pam Dauber, who played Mindy, was the other genius. Robin could change a scene a hundred times with his outrageous antics, and Pam was right there, giving and taking in the moment, not thrown by Robin's spontaneity. They were a great comedic team. Our Improv group's goal was to be as outrageous as possible and take our comedy to the zenith of our collective talent. The prerequisites were "no-holds-barred" and to have fun. I personally found an outlet for creative energy. I learned to put the Om in comedy... to go with the flow of self-discovery.

♥♥♥

Imagine the thrill of meeting Lucille Ball, my lifetime idol. Not only was she the greatest comedian of my youth, she was a mother and an executive producer. When we met, she held my hand and said, "I've seen you. You have the funnies." I was so taken, I was speechless. It was probably my Academy Award. (Of course the fat lady hasn't sung yet on that topic!) Who would know better than Lucy if I were funny? I had tears in my eyes. "It's because of you. It's because of watching you. You were one of my great teachers. Thank you," I gushed.

Another time, I was in Lucy's acting class, an exhilarating experience for me, and a one-time-only rare occasion. A young, heavy-set woman who was starring in a TV show complained to Lucy, "I'm always typecast as a fat lady. I never get different kinds of parts." Lucy winced, "Aren't you a fat lady? Haven't you created your niche? Be grateful, because there are three fat ladies right beyond you ready to jump into your place."

Wanna-Be A U-tube Comedy Star?

Pick a subject you are interested in that you can have fun with: Kids in Diapers, Walking tightropes. DA.

♥ Observe as many situations in real life or in your imagination on your subject, as you can.

♥ Pick your favorite observations. Start with warm-up example and say the story out loud. Practice in front of a mirror. You become your best audience- a good start.

♥ Now you're ready to take your funnies to your family, friends, and the mailman. Reactions? Do you get a laugh? Practice on pets, they are a truthful telltale. If they snore, whoops, it's time to amp up your act!

♥ Keeping adding details, keep practicing, until you get a five-minute routine.

♥ Make an HD video. Put it up on U-Tube,

"I LOVE MY LIFE"

"All the other ones are taken".

I learned from the comedy greats how to do Improv comedy. George Burns taught me one of the most fundamental lessons in comedy. I had been invited to *audition for Mr. Burns to play his niece on a TV* special. The show promised to be a major stepping-stone for me because every great comedian would be there, from Bill Cosby to Steve Martin and everyone in-between.

Mr. Burns wanted to see an array of characters, so being the hardhead that I was; I included my imitation of Marlon Brando and Moe from the Three Stooges. With my knees wobbling in awe of this comic legend, I started my act beneath his cigar smoke-screen. I imitated Marilyn Monroe, Goldie Hawn, mimicked Bette Midler, Carol Burnett (mugging and all), saved the best for last Brando.

Mr. Burns began coughing loudly, so I stopped in mid-sentence. He looked at me and grunted, "Go into the powder room." I was stunned. He said, "Go...go, look in the mirror and come back and tell me what you see."

I went to the ladies room. I was ready to cry. I just stood there and looked at myself. All I saw was ME. What could I say? When I came back, he started in on me. "You want to work in this town?" Oh, those familiar words.

"You got to look at your face...you are a dame. You don't have a kisser like Carol Burnett; you aren't a rubber face. No mugging with that face. Anyway, my niece is a beauty...she wouldn't do those faces in public. You want to be funny? Gracie was funny. She didn't do any mugging." Then he gave me the ultimate compliment. "You've got the timing, you are funny. Now, what are you doing on Friday?"

"Nothing," I squeaked. "Good," he said. "Go get yourself in a Bob Mackie gown. You'll be my niece." I almost fainted. Then he added with that George Burns twinkle, "If you want to, that is."

My life's journey has been about discovering the authentic self. George Burns was referring to operating from the authenticity within myself that allowed me to present a believable character. There is a range of what authentic means. Interpretations of adages such as, "To thine own self be true," have filled up volumes of books. But, our purpose in exploring the freedom of Self, to act without limitation, hesitation, or unworthiness will require that we suspend our view of ourselves and take a leap into the Improv. Trying on different clothes and characters stretches our imagination of what can be possible to achieve and attain.

Shine like a Star

Taking the stage in your life is Star Time. Use full-out energy with no apologies for being the center of attraction. It's your time to shine and glow. You are on the spot, in the spotlight. It's time to promote YOU, flaunt your talents, and follow your dreams.

Great speakers, politicians, and salespeople often mesmerize with charismatic star-energy. We salivate on their every word, wanting more. Realize universal light force, that magnetizing energy is available for all of us. Even if your natural style is low-key, the awareness of star-quality energy will up your peak performance level in all you do. Cultivate it and use it. . Watch the magnetic energy in others. Practice duplicating magnetism in your own communications Watch their reaction to you.

Live the Improv'

Know when to give and when to take; that is, when to take the stage and act, and when to let go and let someone else take center stage. Sometimes in life, as onstage, you are the star of the story. Other times, you are a bit player.

♥ When you take the stage you are 100% responsible for your performance and the results. Take responsibility for your actions. You can correct, improve, and learn something from the so-called mistake without blame-gaming yourself or others. Improvise a solution or fresh start.

♥ Allow others to make their own mistakes and learn from them. When you give over the stage to someone else, you are not responsible for the way they do it. This is especially true in relationships where codependency can happen when doing the Action for the other person. In business, though, if you are the boss, manager, or supervisor, you are ultimately held accountable for every mistake made by your employees. Trusting you picked the right people can be a challenge - give them a chance to grow through their mistakes.

♥ Trust that not all Action has to be preplanned. Planning certainly plays a critical part in Action, but too much planning creates rigidity, fixation, and limits possibility. Trust the flow.

♥ Learn to Bounce back fast. What looks like a setback can be transformed into a success in a second if you are open, limber, and ready? Bounce high!

♥ Flexibility – if you are a natural leader, it can be freeing to follow an Action someone else has initiated, rather than pushing your own idea. Ease up! If you are usually a follower, learn to lead by initiating a new Action. Step up!

Sometimes people will follow you, sometimes they won't. Some- times things go your way, sometimes they don't. Don't take it personally. One of life's great lessons: Detachment comes from looking at life as a great play.

Keys to Improv

♥ Be in the moment. Listen with your entire being – your eyes, hair, nose, and ears.

♥ Let the other person speak, and then listen to what comes out of your mouth. It may be outrageous or nonsensical. Have fun.

♥ Trust. There is no right or wrong. It's about discovery in the moment.

Off The Wall

Imagine stepping out of your own persona for a moment and being someone completely different. Look at life as an Improv game. Take off your habits, quirks, and personality traits have been developed and clung to by your little ego (that resists being so much more).

Choose to strip down to your bare truth, hang-up familiar habits and instantly adopt a new wardrobe and new traits. I enjoyed playing a waitress and dumping meatballs on Chevy Chase on The Flip Wilson Show, or tripping down the steps with Elvira at our workshop, or garbling gibberish in another role as an Italian lady batting cockroaches off the wall (and off the wall it was).

Improv' – The Happy Ticket

Be a Machine: Three people (in a group) come together to play this game. One at a time, each person makes a movement and sound to create a machine. Notice how each person's sound and movement complements the other parts and transforms the machine as a whole. You'll learn how this exercise reflects life in general, as we are a unique part of our family, work, and community as a whole.

Talk out of Both Sides of Your Mouth:

One person stands between two people and carries on two different conversations with both people at once. The two partners pick their own subject, not revealing it, until the game starts. They speak continuously without stopping. **Timeframe: 3 minutes.**

Considerations: Trust you can multi-task. Answer your first response. Don't get caught up in one conversation for too long. Commit to listening and carrying on two conversations. Switch places until each person has had a turn in the middle.

Get Real – From Laughter to Tears

Everyday occurrences from the ludicrous to the sublime test our ability to be in equilibrium and get real – or to bounce off the walls and crash to the ground. At a fundraiser at Mimi's ranch for aged horses, Merrie Way Community donated Peace Smarts manuals, and I agreed to assist in the live auction. Before going on stage, I took a quick trip to the bathroom to freshen up. Yippes!

The unthinkable happened. While at the sink, a temporary cap on my front tooth popped off and whisked down the drain. Staring in the mirror at my toothless grin, I felt like Emma Lutz, my wacky character on TV. I started to laugh, guffawed, bellowing into tears. Then I took notice, only one eye was tearing, a trifling observation.

After discreetly summoning Mimi, we used chopsticks in an attempt to retrieve the lost tooth. As I watched Mimi, a stuntwoman, confidently jabbing the sticks down the drain, a quiet peace swept over me. Gently breathing, I was filled with a joyous feeling. My prima donna, have-to- look-good side took a needed break. All kinds of sugarplum solutions danced in my head: doing the auction without the tooth, going home immediately, or sitting in a darkened corner, out of sight.

Finally, with the help of an off-duty police officer who was on the premises, the tooth magically appeared by opening the drain. Oddly enough, he had watched me on TV playing Emma and felt it was surreal, like we were in a zany episode of the show. We had a great laugh, and I was able to show gratitude by offering a Peace Smarts manual and signing it: "To my hero for the night."

And what was that one eye tearing about? I finally concluded it was a right brain / left-brain balance, and that going with the flow is a great release valve.

Playing In the Shadow and Light

Imagine Marge Simpson morphing into Homer...and Homer with his caustic delivery morphing into Marge. It is the dance of the shadow self and the light self. Some of us deny our shadow self and ignore its vital teaching. Light does not exist without darkness. Let's play with shadows and prance in the light.

♥ Define who is light and who is dark. Pick your character. Choose an issue or topic. Improv. Speak one at a time. Listen. Don't judge. Play it to the hilt, and then switch roles.

♥ "Only the shadow knows." Sunlight plays tricks with shadows. Walking down the street, I love gazing at my shadow – sometimes it is squat and dwarfish, other times it's like the lanky cartoon character Olive Oil. Some of us hide behind the shadows in life, afraid of the dark side.

♥ Stand in the sun on a sidewalk. Spot your shadow. Notice the outline, the size, and its position in relation to where you are standing. Is it bigger, smaller, amazing? Begin walking. Are you following your shadow? Is it to the side of you or behind you?

♥ I do finger shadows on the wall, shaping birds, gremlins, fairies. Characters are magically alive on the wall's canvas, becoming friends to talk and play with.

Out of the womb's watery shadow, they said I was born laughing. The lesson: allowing a smile, through the hurts and disappointments. A two-sided coin: Crying releases laughter. Laughter releases the tears.

Cheesy HAHA - For Fun Create Laughter

For years as a comedy player, my playground was to create the funnies: laughter, giggles, and joy. What a blessed way to earn a living! Do the "Cheesy HAHA" to release physical and emotional tight-spots and to lighten the load. Laughter is contagious, outrageous, and to tally divine. So, let's have a go.

> **Say the word Cheese as many ways as possible.** Keep saying it until you have a feeling of knowingness, a smile of recognition, or until it becomes a Giggle, the familiar precipitator of laughter. Practice the Cheesy Giggle until it becomes a natural, guttural response. Do it until your jaw hurts. Do it through your tears. It's hard to hold on to any- thing after a good laugh or cry. One can lead to the other. Let it rip.

Laugh through pain, HAvoc and HAssles, and grow into HArmony and HAppiness. Laughter is a stress-buster, a tranquilizer without side effects. A good chuckle releases tension, lowers stress hormones, and boosts immune system. Laughter blast through tears and dump anguish.

THE PLAY OF LIFE

"Your Talent Lies in Your Choice"

Stella Adler, famed acting coach of Marlon Brando, was critiquing me. "Why are you wearing those clod- hopper shoes?"

She railed at me, "The character is a dilettante, nota farmer's daughter." Bug-eyed, I drew a blank. Stella penetrated my stupor, "Dah-ling, don't you know, your talent lies in your choice!" Choice meant the character's intention, mannerisms – knowing their emotional score. For an actor, this is a key lesson to contemplate.

Making precise choices on stage trickled into my daily awareness and translated into, "Your talent in life lies in choosing how you live it." What you eat determines your health; the company you choose, choices you make in business, or choosing a mate influence your lifestyle.

The power of choice is the foundation of creativity. Within you are dynamic, powerful energies that make things happen, propelling change. Every moment, how we act, react, and interact with the people and events in our lives is based on our free will to choose. We create our existence from moment-to-moment, manifesting, expanding, learning, and growing. The most important talent you have in living your life is expressing your innate, energetic force. Bounce out of the norm. Lift off the limitations you place on yourself and how you define yourself; mom, dad, son, plumber, CPA. Be creatively centered. No matter what or who we are, we are creative transformers.

You are the expert of your life. You are trained to be the expert. The process involves looking at of all of your experiences, within and without. Choose the best - leave the rest. One way to achieve this is to renew your commitment to change and grow. People I've known who don't take action have weak commitment and believe they can't succeed. You really CAN change your ways. If you follow your flow, your heart within, an enlightened transformation is inevitable. Life is a rhythmic sequence of moments strung together. The beats are more than a simple drum roll; they resound with the pulsation of the life force. When you're in step, in that rhythm, joy and health are bountiful.

Rhythms of HArmony – A Healer

The Mayans said, "The world sings us into being, and we are its song." Your sweet melody and rhythm can illuminate your world. From the natural rhythm of your heartbeat (that is always with you), to the magnificent seasonal changes (the rhythm of a storm, hard or gentle), rhythms are part of nature's symphony.

One morning I heard a loud swoosh. Caught by the unusual sounds I gazed out of the window. To my delight, two Mallard ducks were swimming in the pool. I watched the gentle rhythm as they paddled, gliding across the water as if on glass. The serene images filled my day with gentleness. I practiced gliding through the day like a graceful duck. I enjoyed donning the duckling rhythm of swimming, and I even attempted waddling.

Be mindful of rhythms: Observe the rhythm of flames on a grill, hum of your computer. Listen to the flutter of leaves, the stillness of the moment, the silent rhythm. Creative observation: Whether drinking a cup of tea or writing a weekly report, allow total absorption in rhythm of the activity. Joy and excellence live together in HArmony. **This is Meditation in Action.**

♥ ♥ ♥

JOANNE is an awesome example of creative observation and communing with people, animals, and nature's bounty. Whenever I feel blue, uninspired, or even if I feel great, she lifts my spirit higher with one of her awesome encounters. On her majestic retreat site in Hawaii, she tends a meddlesome goat, chases off intruding wild pigs, and peacefully watches her sheep graze the overgrowth on the land. She dines on the property's succulent papayas and mango's, savoring the fresh Noni juice (an anti-aging elixir). What a life!

From swimming in rhythm with the dolphins to listening to the sound of whales pounding their tales in the ocean like drumrolls, she hears, tastes, and smells the beauty in life. She breathes in the invigorating morning mist. Even in downtown Los Angeles, she'll be the one to hear the feral kitty's cry from under a stoop, pick it up, cuddle it until it purrs and licks her face. Take heart from Joanne's creative observation and embrace nature's bountiful rhythms and HArmony.

Musical Rhythms – Morph Moods

Musical rhythms and tonal frequencies can change attitudes, emotions. Musical modalities are effectively used in treatments for a variety of physical and psychological ailments. Notice daily internal rhythms: when you feel rushed, sluggish, anxious or happy. Be mindful of your breath's rhythm from slow to hyperventilating.

In this particular exercise, you can experiment with music as your healing agent for the heart, body, and mind. A friend had a raging headache. Together we rhythmically breathed into the pain, and then dropped into Silence. A miraculous, calm resonance penetrated, every molecule listened, shifting frequency – the pain gently melted away.

Rigidity vs. Creativity

Are you rigid? If so, in what area? Maybe it feels comfortable and familiar. Do you ever feel, "It's okay just the way it is? Who has time to start over and learn the new stuff?" Whatever happened to spontaneity? Do you have a childlike wonder that just dives in and asks questions later? Remember a moment when spontaneity reigned in your life. Were you seemingly reckless, putting the expected on hold?

The coin flip of rigidity is creativity. The truth is – creativity resides within everyone. The myth is – creativity is a reserved gift of the genius, the artist, or children. Who said there is only one right way to do something? Who said that creativity is meant only for children with curious minds or an artist on a scaffle painting the Sistine Chapel? As long as we are breathing we are creating in the moment. We make choices what to wear, what to eat- to butter our bread or to eat it dry. If you hear a rigid voice, "You can't sing, dance, or frolic with the dolphins"- pay no heed. Sing, dance and frolic with the dolphins and the voice will be dimmed - it will no longer dictate your path.

No matter how old you are, you can keep the childlike wonder of creativity alive. This scintillating pulsation resides inside of you. Creativity is a blast of invention, trial and error, taking risks to grow, to dream, to bring the impossible into possibility, playful and flowing. This zone of expanded awareness is where genius resides. It is not afraid of mistakes; it learns, experiments, and corrects. Albert Einstein failed often, yet he plunged on with steadfast purpose and concentration, without apology. He spoke of a magical power of infinite intelligence that supersedes facts. We can capture creativities truth with one breath so powerful, so mysterious, so gratifying. When in doubt I wear a cap that reads, Einstein.

♥ **Pick three different rhythms**: slow dance to a ballad, a faster rhythm, such as swing/blues, and the fastest – a rumba or hard rock.

♥**Play for three to five minutes.** Sway, clap, dance, or move to the tempo. Become absorbed in the rhythm. Note how each one changes your mood and physical sensations.

♥ **Use your physiology to help you**. When stressed, practice the slower rhythm. When sluggish move to the medium rhythm, build up to faster Beat. When over-charged, use the faster mode to release, and then switch to the slower rhythm to relax.

♥♥♥

Watch a small child at play. Notice how every object, sound, or person they come into contact with produces a creative moment. They touch, smell, feel – closing their eyes while examining something new, and brim with zeal when pursuing an undertaking. This childlike art of approaching the moment with discovery is the essence of creativity.

♥ Appreciation, discovery, insight, and intuition are natural creative impulses. Morphing constricting attitudes toward yourself will teach you how to develop inspiration and to achieve a refreshing point of view. Rigidity is limited perspective... Have courage and take a risk... Do one thing you find daring. Climb the mountain, buy that paintbrush... Transformation is a Bounce away...

Bounce Into Freedom

Do you have a recording studio or padded workout room in your home, chances are this isn't an option. The next best thing is a Bouncy for Fun; those bright colored room-sized tents – a kid's jump-fest.

At a kid's birthday party, my curiosity was up so I mustered mega courage to plunge into a bouncy tent. With shoes off, I struggled through the net door, closed my eyes and jumped into a heap of writhing bodies, rolling over on top or under, a foot, arm, or tummy. After about thirty seconds of shouts and giggles (being the average socialized adult), fun turned to fear of being bopped, socked, or bit by a roly-poly kid. I got over it by laughing – a lot.

Find a bouncy in an amusement park or at a kid's party. A trampoline is a safer bet for the timid and still gives a good bounce and releases tension, building energy. How about bouncy boots, a wild contraption I tried. You strap them on and bounce a foot high or so, leaping for- ward like a frog. Truly not for klutzes, you will surely land on you butt. I did. At least give a bouncy a chance and play like a kid again.

Cherub Within

Dreaming: I was on a train riding next to a very tall man. He wore a long-coat, trimmed goatee, top hat; reminiscent of day's gone by. He nodded pleasantly and I got off at my stop. That evening coming home the same man was on the train...intrigued I debarked when he did and followed him up the winding cobble stone street to where he lived. Sitting on a bench nearby, I pondered why I had done such a silly thing as to follow someone I didn't know.

Then quick Flashes of a tiny man, less than three feet tall bounced out the same house. Filled with exuberance, he approached me and literally jumped onto my lap. "Merrie Lynn, I am so happy to see you. Where have you been?" Smiling with a cheerful glee he hopped back onto to the ground sparkling with joy and laughter. I felt a free childlike energy fill me with wonder.

I could see he was the same man, the one on the train and the cherub child before me. How amazing a reflection of the adult...over riding the joyous child within.

Release Cherub Within

Do you wear an adult persona with an appropriate human mask... who enters the world daily, carrying on as YOU? In the meantime, inside your heart a gleeful cherub is dancing, singing, and having fun. Yet, the restraints of our long coats bind and keep us from experiencing that exhilarating joy. Overtime our cherub hides, shrinks, and maybe we ignore its essence. It acts out to get our attention: with an occasional temper tantrum, an over the top exhilaration, popping the lid off of our repressed self.

Where is your childlike wonder? Is it at play, alive and well in you? Are you balancing responsibilities with joy?

♥ Laugh out loud everyday. Watch funny movies.

♥ Hangout with a sense of humor, have fun.

♥ Get off the serious, onto the real. Life is not a drag we make it so. Give yourself permission, do the ridiculous, hula-hoop, belly dance, balance a ball on your nose.

♥ Do what you love. From catching butterflies to rollerblading, or catching the wave on a boogie board.

♥ Eat cotton candy, blow bubbles...Who is squelching the Cherub kid within? Got it... Share fun with fun folks.

Wake-UP... Your Heart's Melting

At any stage in life you can melt your heart, let down your guard, and flow into your natural state of Being. Depending on what and why you shut down, the opening can feel as if you are a newborn. By embracing the newness each step taken is gentler and your vulnerability feels precious and alive. This awakening is timed for expansive growth, whether you wanted it or were unconscious of its coming, it arrives right on time. It is you unfolding, as you are destined, and you are no longer afraid of change and you are no longer capable of holding rigidity in your heart of hearts.

What Is This Awakening?

Awakening is a quantum awareness, an internal and external glimpse of evolving possibility. You begin to think new thoughts and embrace new actions. By watching your actions, old behavioral patterns take a back row seat, no longer remaining an obstacle in your path. In this multi-dimensional awareness, tenderness, openness, and expansiveness lead to a fresh emotionally connected state of being. Emotions are there to touch your humanness, and you drop defensive that have controlled you. Other people may perceive a change in you?" You seem more relaxed' "You're glowing, are you in love/' YES! It is a Love state and it is yours, so personal and divine. It is the crack in the cosmic egg, the seedling that will unfold new ways of seeing and BEing.

Some of us feel the spark of the divine operating through us. We are catapulted into a new reality. This dynamic energy force has always been there even when we were shut down. With an heightened awareness we recognize everything is temporal, yet eternal, and that everyday life is in constant flux whether we can see or feel its movement and expansion.

How to maintain this state of Awareness depends on your willingness to see the signs, the guideposts of information and connection with your inner most truth. Trying to hold on to this newness can be a trap; it's not about holding on to anything, it's allowing and accepting 'all of it' to be, just as it is. This flow state of mind gently spills over into what you think, what you say, and how you behave.

The trigger of your awakening can come in a jolt, or it can arrive after a series of events, conversations, or a inexplicable synchronicity that explodes into Newness. Often the explosion is subtle and it shows up as life's sweetness, feeling 'Good for no reason'.

In this bombastic world of overly charged emotions, remaining in a neutral zone will help you flow, free of fear, living in the adventure of Newness.

Spend a few moments deep breathing into the silence. Under a starlit sky you can feel the expansiveness of this eternal wonder. Know you are part of this universal greatness, riding and risking adventure, inspiring every step you take.

Creative Late Bloomer

Grandma Moses started painting at 87, a stellar example that within us lies untapped treasures. Rocket-launch an opportunity you may have left behind, an interest or potential talent that lies dormant. It's never too late to take up the guitar, the piano, carpentry, dance. Creative exploration stimulates your brain's development and enriches life in unexpected ways.

Excuses don't fly in our Improv' world...we soar on the wings of trust. Not buying into excuses..."Can't do it." "Don't have the talent." "Don't like the task." "It's not worth it." "Not interested." Inability to take Action weakens self-esteem. Choosing a negative value judgment brings on a lack of inspiration and motivation. Write a message in your Heart. Imagine what could be. Pure, healing, elated joy... So it IS!

What ignites the creative, the Loveforce, magical living? Unlock the mystery of PLAY. Participate right NOW! Gaze at your palm: designs crisscrossing, patterning unique expression. Breathe deep. Look closer at the swirls of wonder, imprinting your specialness. Take creative YOU into all you see, feel, do, and say.

HaHa Healers

"I finally got the feeling we're all ONE...when they raised our taxes."

A 98-year-old woman dedicated her life to laughter. She memorized jokes and shared her funnies with everyone she met. She would laugh so hard at her own jokes that she became known as an inspirational Laugh Track. Up until her final breath she spread her contagious joy, healing with HAHA's. Laughter enlivens us, and it's a proven healing agent. .It loosens the mind and spawns creativity via the brain-laughter connection. In the same way the brain muscle can be developed through chess, our brain has funny-bone muscles. Laughter pumps dopamine, a feel-good reward system chemical near the base of the skull. MRI brain scans have shown the blood flow in areas of the brain that produce intuition are the same areas of the brain that induce laughter.

Laughter can sharpen and recalibrate intuition, playing a role in social decision-making. Lighten-up; keep those gut-level hunches on target. Winds of laughter fill the day...when you open to your blessings.

Angel Wings... FLY

Could you, did you, can you spot an Earth Angel if you see one? TaDa! They come in all sizes, shapes, colors, and species. Granted our pets are sent here to watch over us...they love us unconditionally 24/7, as we are, with all our great points and flaws.

Ever meet someone... and bada-boom there's a chill to the bone, a tingle of recognition like you always knew they were coming? They hang around just long enough to spin you 180 degrees onto a new path. These are your life-changing Angels, who shower you with a breathlessness that quiets your being, or jumpstarts a racing mind, attempting to make sense of it. This multidimensional encounter is beyond reason. It encourages emotional release. It inspires an enlivened physical and psyche awareness that brings clarity of purpose, a shift in your perceptions, and a willingness to seek transformation and change.

Angels show up for different reasons. For instance, they appear in the investment world and plop down the seed money, or fund a project. They are literally called Angels, most likely because the gesture feels heaven sent. Whether heaven sent or earthly bound, spiritual or material energy is all one energy field. When we unknowingly separate the two, we juggle in the balance, we remain impotent or confused about how to claim our good and to enjoy a great life.

Angels have a common thread, they teach us lessons.. Whether a spouse or friend, they touch our heart and soul. As great teachers, they assist us in removing our blocks and walls of resistance. Often they appear as an adversary; a grumpy boss, a rebellious teen, a discontented spouse. They seemingly wear devil horns, tossing thorns and bristles our way. The tender, loving ones create a comfort zone, just by being in their presence we feel honored and accepted for who we truly are. With perceptive knowing they recognize our potential and operate from that premise. They sense our innate perfection and innate potential, regardless of our state of consciousness.

Our most significant Angels are our children...they come to us to bring all the LOVE. They begin innocently, loving unconditionally...then life hits them in the face with obstacles that put limiting conditions in their psyche. Time flies and they grow up...we are those children, YOU and ME....and the cycle of opportunity begins again.

We are all Angels in Training...everyday provides an opportunity to perform 'acts of kindness' to be there in full measure for someone in need. Lend a listening ear, go the extra mile to help, bring over Chicken Soup, or give a hug and smile.

MerrieWay's Call to Action: Bring out the Angel in You...and be willing to be an Angel Spotter, each day. "You're an Angel" is a gratitude salutation worth its weight in gold.

I Love Me

'I love Me' is not a narcissist's mantra. It's the highest level of coming to terms with who you are. I can honestly say 'I love me.' There is no one I would trade places with on this earth...for all the tea in China, vodka in Russia, or gold bullion. Can't sell this soul to the devil's lure. Don't want anyone's else's head space, karma, physical body, central nervous system, or whatever. Happy with me!

Choose to acknowledge and speak to your self, "Love you're here." You can connect to multiple aspects of self, the wondrous child, your outrageous teen, wise mother or father, sensuous lover, powerful woman or man. I often say to my self, "I love you Merrie Lynn" or "You are so much fun to be with."

Loving spending time with yourself and appreciating who you are with all your foibles, brings adventure into moments that would seem blasé and go unnoticed.

Speak to yourself out loud, preferably when you are alone, or in your head voice while going through your daily activities. Say to yourself, "I love Me....use your name. Repeat it when you are simply being present with yourself.

SHADOW SELF... ALTER EGO FUMING

"Gag Me," my alter ego shouted, "you sound like Tweedy Bird on a manic love-fest. How about when sell your self short and you're on overwhelm? You're grueling in boring and self-loathing and admit it, you're in major dislike. Will you honestly belt out, "I don't like myself." I felt like a shrinking violet on that note... I looked inside at my Swiss-cheese guts, filled with holy doubt. then I muttered to that haunting ego... 'What happens to 'I love me?'

Loving and liking are two different animals. We know that, you can love someone and not like them. One is a pussycat, a loving roly-poly, and the other is a down and dirty tigress, which can recriminate, judge and, criticize with disdain. It's in the moment. Hey, some corrections of bad habits need to be conquered, but not at the expense I hate myself, I'm worthless. That is a lie... in that moment if you remember your self-esteem or worth. Change the parts that bug you.

That means getting out of the mind fog that keeps you in limbo, in general anxiety and overwhelm.

Brain Fog... is physical prison, it may be bio=chemical, veering on depression. lack of nutrients sunshine and fun.

The challenge is when you don't like yourself. You can love and dislike someone. Catch recriminating yourself...this is the time nip it or recognition, that once again self-talk is high leveled communication...it's the judge speaking, the annihilator, or the debater, or illuminating coach. Catch the put-down swiftly and dialogue back, settling inner discrepancies. "Thank you for pointing out I am sloppy waxing the car, guess I'll need more patience." "I love me for working it out."

Celebrate Yourself – It's Your World

You are the center of your universe. Like the sun, people rotate around you like planets and moons. This is not narcissism; it is honoring your truth self, your bliss, all THAT IS. When bored, entertain yourself. Skip for a fun boost. Play with irreverence about something silly you won't actually do. I imagined I was trolling birthday parties snagging balloons for my next party.

"Laugh 'Til I Thought I'd Die"

Back in the day, three laughing holy men traveled the countryside creating laughter among the villagers. Their contagious lightness of being promoted healing, cured sadness, and dissolved discontent and woe. During an auspicious holiday in the midst of a laughing jag, one of the holy men died. Without missing a beat, the other two holy men continued laughing hysterically.

Appalled, the villagers cried, "How can you laugh? This is no way to mourn. How irreverent, so sacrilegious." The holy men answered, "We are laughing in his honor. He lived to laugh and his spirit laughs on in joy."

Determined to give a proper burial, the villagers set forth with a creation ceremony. The holy men relayed their friend's final request: in the middle of town - they honored his last request.

"For my departure, make sure it is sundown and do not touch my clothes." All agreed to follow his wish. As they lit the funeral pyre, two remaining holy men rolled in laughter, celebrating their friend's down their faces, melting away all meaning of misperceived loss and judgment.

Inspired by the wise men, I decided to bring love and laughter in my booties, every step along the way. There is a vibrating cord of life – a magical connection of playing life to the fullest. This is the time...Play.

♥ **Bucket List?** Fun, meaningful things to do before you die. How about calling it your Dream List and Living it NOW? From riding in the back of pick-up, to making a collage of four leaf clovers, to the more exotic, making love in a Gondola on the Venice canal, or paying back money borrowed to a long lost friend. The list is as long as or short as your Imagination. Keep it going... Dream.

CHAPTER 7

MerrieWay Q & A

♥Bring On The Happy♥

Touch your nose, reach your toes, share your heart... sniff a rose. Life's a miracle... Joy!

Let's start with your questions. You have generalized malaise, or the blues, anxiety that you can't put your focus on. It seems overwhelming to sense why you're in a downspin or why your predicament remains elusive. In this state of mind fog, it's helpful to reach out for a friend or family member for counsel. What if the problem is your friend? What if your friends are too self-involved to be there for you? Funny Wise Woman is here to hear...and jumpstart your solution.

Merrie Lynn Ross' credentials: MerrieWay lemonade stand began when I was 8-years-old. My brother and I set-up shop on the corner of our street. This became the cool action spot. Why? I soon realized a big smile and a listening ear sold lemonade. I made friends from 2-90 and a newfound compassion for others and their concerns. As the years passed, I found my heart gravitating to those in need, desiring a kind word, gesture, or hug.

Does it sound all too simple to 'Bring On the Happy"? Today more than ever, we need practical, common sensical, doable solutions. We need a direction or new perspective to simply lift out of the forest and capture more than the limited purview of trees.

Justin, a 19-year-old college frosh asks: "I just found out, a girl I was seeing in high school is five months pregnant. She told my best friend I was the father. I could be. What should I do?"

MerrieWay: I could suggest taking the next train out of town and never looking back. But...that's a cop-out. So let's look at the real possibility. You can avoid this, wait until the baby is born and then take a DNA test to determine if you are the father. Or you could contact her and preferably meet face-to-face find out what she is feeling about having a child, alone, or what are her intentions?

Obviously you broke up for a reason. Do you still care for each other? You are both young and just beginning your life course. Other factors come into play. Was she seeing other people during your relationship or were you the only one she was sexually active with? Parenting a child at any age is a lifetime commitment. She may not intend on keeping the child and if you are the father how would you feel about adoption? Seek advice from your family, a counselor, or professional advisor would be best. Becoming anxious will not solve the dilemma, getting the facts at this juncture is vital. Blessings, keep us posted. ml

Rebecca Shares: It's hard for me to admit I've gained 30 pounds, I'm a single mom and I just got a new job. Stress is making me feel like running away from my problems. What should I do?

Merrie Lynn: You know what you won't do, don't you? That's a clue what to do. You won't leave your children and you are proving yourself – to be a good Mom. You work and carry your responsibility. You didn't mention if the father is a support or if you have family back up. No matter, you do need some support, emotionally as well as physically to handle your life. Eating is one way to comfort, when you feel alone, anxious, and food becomes your emotionally reliable friend.

Visit LightHeart Path: www.merrieway.com Learn simple and powerful LightHeart Breath technique.

♥ **Practice LightHeart Breath** when you are going to gobble up something that is comfort food. Do it when you feel anxious, tired, or stressed. In time, you will see the triggers that cause you to turn to food.

♥ **Have fun.** What do you enjoy? Include your kids, swim, hike, get outside and breathe. Learn the HAHA's. Share it with you kids too. Laugh and Breathe. A true vibrational Uplift.

Lavern Writes: Merrie Lynn, I am so grateful you are here and how you inspire so many of us. We lost our home last year, due to a fire and our insurance didn't cover full replacement. Now my husband has a leg injury and he can't work. I work at home and he and I are at odds over every ridiculous thing. My nerves are shot.

Merrie Lynn: You have determined what you argue about is ridiculous. Let's carry that to an extreme. If you could get your humor about life in gear, there might be some surprising changes. Instead of getting caught up in a debate, "I'm right" stance. Look at the absurd, the ridiculous, and the insignificance of the battles.

♥ What's underneath the quarrels? How does your husband feel about being home so much? Does he feel useless, bored, angry? Decide you are not supporting a debate team any longer and tell him.

♥ Find mutual things you like and do them. Time for a creative boost... massage, cuddling, watching the sunset alone, and then together, is a good thought.

♥ Meditate, jog...remember why you married and I suggest that he do the same.

ADDITIONAL RESOURCES

BOOKS BY MERRIE LYNN ROSS

Bounce Off The Walls- Land On Your Feet

Happy Heart Journal

Adventures of Funny Mummy

The Bully Project – Peace-Makers

Peace Smarts

Morph America

Nartikki

Products and Courses/Workshops

Peace Smarts Within ...E-Course with MP3's /mini book

HAHA Healers Teleseminar, E-Course , Live Workshops

Life As An Improv' - E-course, MP3's + Bonus Tele-seminar.

MerrieWay Offers Free cutting edge info'- expert tools. What are your questions around biz' building, health, wealth, family concerns? Ask. We'll help on the solution track

Merrie Lynn is available for media interviews, live events, lectures, motivational speaker engagements, and workshop

www.merrieway.com

www.merriewayday.com

www.bounceoffthewalls.com

ABOUT THE AUTHOR

Merrie Lynn Ross – award winning writer/ filmmaker/actor has starred in 35+ TV/films. Best known as daytime's first comedienne, she giggled into millions of viewer's hearts on 'General Hospital'. Internationally acclaimed as a child advocate, honored by Presidents' Clinton and George W, she created "Morph America" and "Peace Smarts" curriculums: helping over two million families to create a peace culture.

After suffering a personal tragedy and rediscovering a way back to living in purpose, Merrie Lynn was guided to share her healing and life altering recipes. With a contagious joyous energy she proves to be a beacon of light for everyone she meets.

She currently stars on 'MerrieWay Day' TV - filled with uplifting news, red-carpet folly, and fun global treks. Dedicated to empower youth, she's producing the film, "Franky…What's Next?" written by Byron Fox – to be used in tandem with "Peace Smarts".

A hill-dweller in Southern California, Merrie Lynn lives with her two shelties, and enjoys a 'green healthy' life with her circle of loving friends.

Enjoy this FREE GIFT

BYRON'S SERIES

BE REAL, LAUGH & LOVE

BE Real, Laugh and Love's Inspirational content will be sent to you with instructions. An amazing way into your heart's desire and how to actualize your Truth.

GO to ~ www.BeRealLaughLove.com

Dear Friends,

I offer you a big Hug and two-thumbs up for sharing ' Life As An Improv' and for journeying on the sacred path of HAHA Healers.

As Soul-Pods... we are swimming in this vast sea of life. Connecting in wisdom, growing in joy as our destiny unfolds.

"Follow your heart." Listen to your heart – it has a mind of its own. When your mind and heart are in a tug of war it indicates you don't know what you want. If you feel a tugging at your heartstrings or your mind, step back before acting. Pause. Ask clarifying questions. When leading from the heart's intelligence your life's purpose blooms, continuously expanding. You live in harmony and loving relationships are more easily attained. May you flow in grace and gentle calm.

Heartfelt blessings to... **"BE Real, Laugh & Love"**.

Made in the USA
San Bernardino, CA
19 December 2012